RAPP & RAPP
Architects

CHARLES WARD RAPP

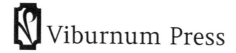
Viburnum Press

On the cover, clockwise from top right: C. W. and George L. Rapp (Rapp Collection); Chicago Theatre 1921 facade (Rapp Collection); I. H. and W. M. Rapp (Rapp Collection); New Mexico Building construction (1915) at the San Diego Fair (Courtesy Palace of the Governors Photo Archive [NMHM/DCA] negative #060255); New Mexico Territorial Capitol (1900), Santa Fe (Fletcher Collection).

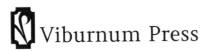

Viburnum Press

www.virburnumpress.com

www.rappandrapparchitects.com

Book design by Erin VanWerden

DEDICATION

To the memory of the principals and staff of Isaac Rapp, Edwards & Rapp,
Bulger & Rapp, Thomas & Rapp, I. H. & W. M. Rapp, I. H. & W. M. Rapp
and A. C. Hendrickson, I. H. & W. M. Rapp and Francis W. Spencer,
C. W. & Geo. L. Rapp and Rapp & Rapp, Architects, from 1855 to 1965.

TABLE OF CONTENTS

AUTHOR'S PREFACE

Though much work of the Rapp architects across the country has been well recorded, publicized and protected by landmark status, the architects themselves are not so well known. This book is the first to tell their story. The late historian Joseph Duci Bella of the Theatre Historical Society of America persistently encouraged a book about the architects, their lives and how they worked, referring to the subject as "the last piece of the Rapp & Rapp puzzle."

The need for a Rapp book had been clear for years but there never seemed enough supporting information. The architects, unaware that they were making history, left only a thin paper trail, hardly spoke publicly and rarely were quoted in newspapers. They simply worked, kept up professional contacts and let their buildings speak for themselves. The movie palaces built by C. W. & Geo. L. Rapp's Chicago office during the 1920s were appreciated from the start and even more so in recent years, but aside from a signature "Santa Fe Style" the work of their brothers I. H. & W. M. Rapp, Trinidad, Colorado seemed lost in the mists of the Old West. As it turned out, nothing was lost, it just hadn't been found, and as the years passed the information needed to tell the Rapp story gained shape. Out of countless interviews, telephone conversations and exchanges of documents and letters, mysteries were solved and questions found answers.

The present book results from years of often-fortuitous contact with individuals listed in the accompanying Acknowledgments and Special Acknowledgments. Very important sources through the long process of collecting oral history were older members of the Rapp family, those who knew the family, and people in the office and their spouses, all of whom are now deceased. Incomparably valuable were the remaining Chicago office records and drawings, given in the 1980s to the Chicago Historical Society, now named Chicago History Museum.

ACKNOWLEDGMENTS

Individuals mentioned below provided invaluable help and information needed to compile this book. They are listed roughly in the order of contribution. Many are now deceased and are so-noted where that is known.

John W. D. Wright, deceased

Evelyn Dumas Brush, deceased

Robert K. Bauerle, deceased

Virginia M. Rapp, deceased

Mrs. Theron Woolson, deceased

Mason Gerardi Rapp, deceased

Mary G. Rapp Laun, deceased

George Hamilton Bunge, deceased

Edwin B. Storako, R&R 1948–1965

Professor John Parrish, University of Illinois

Sigma Chi Fraternity National Headquarters
    William Bringham
    Merrill E. "Boz" Prichard
    Sigma Chi Staff, Evanston, Illinois

Daniel Harmon Brush IV, deceased

Arthur Frederick Adams, deceased

Arthur Frederick Adams, Jr.

Theatre Historical Society of America
    Brother Andrew Corsini Fowler, deceased
    Joseph Duci Bella, deceased
    Steve Levin, deceased
    Bill Benedict, deceased
    Richard Sklennar
    et al

Chicago Historical Society
    Robert Brubaker
    Wim De Wit
    Scott LaFrance

Chicago History Museum
    Rob Medina
    Annie Chase

Francoise Brush Riley

San Diego Historical Society

Herbert J. Peterson, C.P. Clare Co.

Susan McCue Kuester, Ashland, Wisconsin

Barbara Bennett, Carbondale, Illinois

Mrs. Francis J. (Clara) Weirauch Long, R&R 1948–1965, deceased

Peter Hoffman, R&R 1918–1932, deceased

Bret Kelly, Pueblo Colorado

Douglas McHendrie, Denver, Colorado

Katherine L.H. Olson

Jill Hartman, Racine Public Library

Richard Latham

Ken Fletcher, Trinidad, Colorado

Dorothy R. Rapp, deceased

Eric Mason Ellis

Jean Hershner, Charlottesville Paramount

University of Illinois Archives
    Christopher J. Prom

Mary Brush

William L. Powell

Jon Peterson

Robert W. Fulk

William M. Rapp

Patricia B. Clark

Carolyn Rapp Ellis

Gayle Tepper, Rubloff Residential Properties

William J. Clark, Ironton, Ohio

Jennifer L. Rapp Peterson

Stephanie F. Rapp

Dr. Gerald T. Pollard

Dede Lingle Ittner, Carbondale

Colorado Historical Society, Denver

Linda Brandon, Carbondale

Jacqueline T. Rapp

Palace of the Governors, Santa Fe
    Daniel Kosharek
    Nicholas Chiarella

SPECIAL ACKNOWLEDGMENTS

Trinidad, Colorado, researcher and historian Ken Fletcher was first to observe the Rapps to be the only family in history to have produced four noted architects in one generation, followed by three in the next. The statement gains credibility the longer it is pondered. Mr. Fletcher's tireless and ongoing research into the lives and output of two of those architects, I. H. and W. M. Rapp of Trinidad, has been a major contribution to this book, for which he has the author's deepest thanks. The book could not have been finished without Mr. Fletcher.

Special gratitude also is expressed in memory of both Brother Andrew Corsini Fowler and Joseph Duci Bella who provided information and insight concerning the world and work of the Chicago firm of C. W. & Geo. L. Rapp. Brother Andrew and Mr. Duci Bella were among the founders of the Theatre Historical Society of America and were, in this author's view, the most complete historians of cinema architecture.

Additional appreciation is extended to Arthur F. Adams, Jr., for images from the Adams scrapbooks and insights into the career of his father who was chief designer for C. W. & Geo. L. Rapp during the 1920s and 30s. Further thanks are due to all who provided images and illustrations for this book. Most of these sources have been credited, but even after due diligence a few remain unknown. The author will appreciate any clarifying information.

Thanks also to Gerald T. Pollard at Research Triangle Park, Raleigh, for valuable advice and skill in copy editing the book's final draft.

A special thanks must go to Jennifer Rapp Peterson for her expertise on image restoration, art direction and book production.

This book is underwritten by the generous support of William and Jacqueline Rapp.

NOTE TO READER

French spelling for the word "theatre" is applied throughout this book. Rapp & Rapp adhered to this usage in their work, a practice the author has respected.

THE RAPP ARCHITECTS

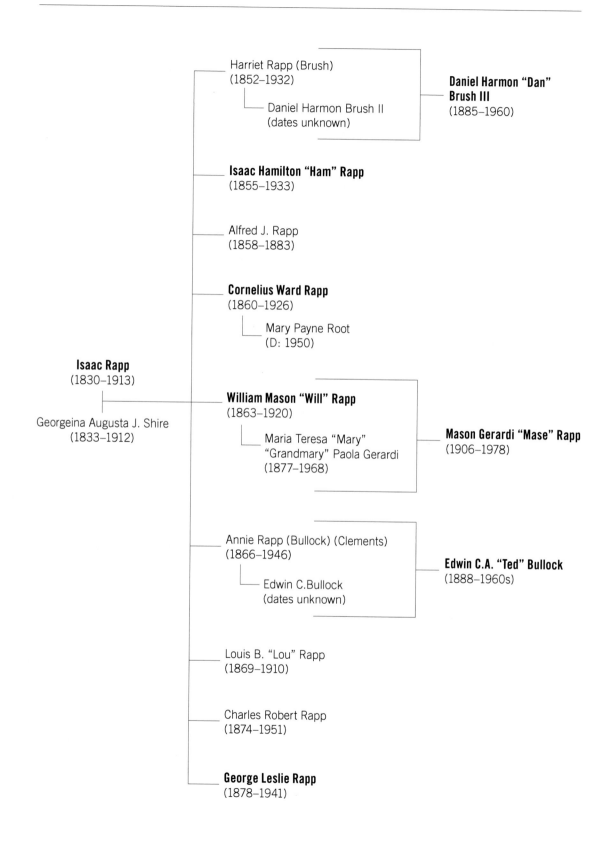

Harriet Rapp (Brush)
(1852–1932)

Daniel Harmon Brush II
(dates unknown)

Daniel Harmon "Dan" Brush III
(1885–1960)

Isaac Hamilton "Ham" Rapp
(1855–1933)

Alfred J. Rapp
(1858–1883)

Cornelius Ward Rapp
(1860–1926)

Mary Payne Root
(D: 1950)

Isaac Rapp
(1830–1913)

Georgeina Augusta J. Shire
(1833–1912)

William Mason "Will" Rapp
(1863–1920)

Maria Teresa "Mary" "Grandmary" Paola Gerardi
(1877–1968)

Mason Gerardi "Mase" Rapp
(1906–1978)

Annie Rapp (Bullock) (Clements)
(1866–1946)

Edwin C. Bullock
(dates unknown)

Edwin C.A. "Ted" Bullock
(1888–1960s)

Louis B. "Lou" Rapp
(1869–1910)

Charles Robert Rapp
(1874–1951)

George Leslie Rapp
(1878–1941)

Color drawing by A. C. Rindskopf

GRAND LOBBY OF THE MICHIGAN THEATRE, DETROIT
C. W. & GEO. L. RAPP, ARCHITECTS

ORGAN SCREEN AND PROSCENIUM ARCH, PARAMOUNT THEATRE, NEW YORK
C. W. & GEO. L. RAPP, ARCHITECTS

GRAND STAIRS AND FOUNTAIN, LOBBY OF THE PARAMOUNT THEATRE, NEW YORK
C. W. & GEO. L. RAPP, ARCHITECTS

AUDITORIUM OF THE PARAMOUNT THEATRE, NEW YORK, SHOWING MEZZANINE, LOGES AND BALCONY
C. W. & GEO. L. RAPP, ARCHITECTS

STUDY IN COLOR OF THE AUDITORIUM, PARAMOUNT THEATRE, NEW YORK
C. W. & GEO. L. RAPP, ARCHITECTS

Color drawing by A. C. Rindskop.

GRAND STAIRS AND LOBBY AS SEEN FROM THE MUSIC ROOM, UPTOWN THEATRE, CHICAGO

C. W. & GEO. L. RAPP, ARCHITECTS

AUDITORIUM OF THE UPTOWN THEATRE, CHICAGO, SHOWING MEZZANINE, LOGES AND BALCONY
C. W. & GEO. L. RAPP, ARCHITECTS

Color drawing by A. C. Rindskopf

VIEW OF THE ORGAN SCREEN AND SURROUNDING TREATMENT, ORIENTAL THEATRE, CHICAGO

C. W. & GEO. L. RAPP, ARCHITECTS

1 | FOOTINGS & FOUNDATIONS

I t's been said that the Rapps of Carbondale, Illinois, were the only family in history to have produced four noted architects in one generation followed by three in the next. Including the first father Isaac Rapp among them would mean that the Rapps' southern Illinois hometown likely is the only city ever to have produced in consecutive generations eight major builders from the same family. Isaac Rapp's buildings were central to Carbondale's development from 1855 while the work of his sons and grandsons came to be represented across the nation.

All the Rapps were first and foremost general commercial architects, meaning they would build anything anywhere for anyone in any style. Despite these generalist tendencies the two separate firms founded by Isaac's sons each contributed a unique architecture for which they are most remembered. For I. H. & W. M. Rapp of Trinidad, Colorado, founded in 1891, the most memorable contribution was a simple and straightforward native Pueblo Revival style that came to be known as the Santa Fe style. Most spectacular of all the Rapp architecture were the movie palaces of the 1920s, which brought enduring fame to the Chicago firm of C. W. & Geo. L. Rapp, Architects, founded in 1907.

It is impossible to overstate the social impact of these Jazz Age movie houses. During the Prohibition years 1919 to 1932 hundreds of imposing cinema castles by the Rapps and many other architects confidently sprang-up across the country in a dizzying series of ambitious projects, representing the first successful experiment in saturation mass entertainment. With their big and rich new theatres, movie studios were able to open films simultaneously from coast to coast. As the Prohibition years were a golden age for movie theatre construction, the following decade of the 1930s was a storied age for the movies themselves. Despite wide economic hardship resulting from the Great Depression movie going was inexpensive public entertainment as giant studios like Paramount,

Isaac Rapp's first son Isaac Hamilton "Ham" Rapp pictured in the 1880s. (Rapp Collection)

William Mason Rapp in 1898. He was Ham's younger brother and partner in the Trinidad, Colorado firm of I. H. & W. M. Rapp. (Rapp Collection)

The Museum of Art, Santa Fe, I. H. & W. M. Rapp's 1916 replication of their San Diego Fair New Mexico Building. The building was dedicated November 24, 1917. This was the prototype Pueblo Revival design that created what came to be known as the Santa Fe Style. (Fletcher Collection)

Warner Brothers, Fox, Metro Goldwyn Mayor and RKO turned-out nearly 700 films a year to fill their glittering theatres, attracting 65 million patrons a week.

Sumptuous settings for stage productions and film exhibition, these palaces were as much a form of show business as the movies themselves. As one movie mogul client Marcus Loew remarked, "I don't sell tickets to movies. I sell tickets to theatres." For Loew, Rapp & Rapp built Brooklyn's Kings Theatre and the Jersey in Jersey City, two of the five advertised "Wonder Theatres" in the New York City area. Chicago's A. J. Balaban of the Balaban & Katz exhibiting company described their Rapp & Rapp theatres as captivating environments within which every patron "would feel like a king."

Greeted by local newspapers with banner headlines, each new theatre was populist architecture exploiting regal motifs. George L. Rapp (1878–1941) wrote a 1925 essay in which democracy was expressed as elevation through elegance for all:

> "Watch the eyes of a child as it enters the portals of our great theatres and treads the pathway into fairyland. Watch the bright light in the eyes of the tired shop-girl who hurries noiselessly over carpets and sighs with satisfaction as she walks amid furnishings that once

With the intimate rose and gold 1915 Al. Ringling Theatre, Baraboo, Wisconsin, C. W. & Geo. L. Rapp set an elegant tone and example for movie palaces built by legions of architects across America during the 1920s. (Rapp Collection)

delighted the hearts of queens. See the toil-worn father whose dreams have never come true, and look inside his heart as he finds strength and rest within the theatre. There you have the answer to why motion picture theatres are so palatial.

"Here is a shrine to democracy where there are no privileged patrons. The wealthy rub elbows with the poor and are better for the contact. Do not wonder, then, at the touches of Italian Renaissance, executed in glazed polychrome terra-cotta, or at the lobbies and foyers adorned with replicas of precious masterpieces of another world, or at the imported marble wainscoting or the richly ornamented ceilings with motifs copied from master touches of Germany, France, Italy, or at the carved niches, the cloistered arcades, the depthless mirrors, and the great sweeping staircases. These are not impractical attempts at showing off. These are part of a celestial city—a cavern of many-colored jewels, where iridescent lights and luxurious fittings heighten the expectation of pleasure. It is richness unabashed, but richness with a reason."[1]

Dedicated to making money by glamorizing the new medium of film, the grand theatres with all their glitter gave context to what it meant to be a movie star. In those days before radio and television, theatres designed by Rapp & Rapp and staffed by ushers precise as military units captivated the entertainment-hungry American public as they flocked into the palaces to ogle and touch all the astonishing opulence George Rapp wrote about. Rapp & Rapp piled grandeur upon elegance as the firm increasingly attracted clients for whom cost was no obstacle. Theatre entrepreneurs learned to spend freely on Rapp projects, expecting and getting their money's worth and more.

The Chicago Rapps built theatres and commercial architecture from Providence to Portland, from Charlottesville to Seattle, and in dozens of cities big and small in between. If you lived in New York you went to Rapp & Rapp's Paramount at Times Square, the Brooklyn Paramount or Loew's Kings. In Washington, D.C. you went to the Fox Theatre in Rapp & Rapp's National Press Club Building. In Omaha, Galesburg and Memphis you went to Rapp & Rapp Orpheums. In Chattanooga there was the Tivoli, in Joliet the Rialto and in Milwaukee and Madison you went to Rapp & Rapp theatres if you went to the movies at all. In Cleveland, Dayton and Cincinnati there were Rapp & Rapp theatres and office buildings built for B.F. Keith, and theatres for Warner Brothers in Milwaukee, West Chester, East Chester and Youngstown. Pittsburgh, St. Paul, Denver, Buffalo, Detroit, Louisville, Wichita, Brookline and still others hosted their own wondrous Rapp & Rapps.[2]

Demand for the firm's work during the 1920s movie palace mania seemed inexhaustible, and during the headiest days George Rapp rarely had to leave the office, as many major movie studio executives and independent exhibitors from across the country walked in the door. Among them were the Greek-American Skouras brothers—Spyros, Charles and George—St. Louis movie exhibitors who began as nickelodeon operators in 1914 and by 1924 ran a fiefdom of forty houses. Familiar with Rapp & Rapp's St. Louis Theatre (1925, converted to Powell Symphony Hall in 1968), they hired the architects to build their crowning Ambassador Theatre (1927). The Skouras brothers' fortunes developed along with the movie industry, ultimately with Charles as president of west coast Fox, George as chairman of United Artists, and Spyros who engineered the merger of Fox with 20th Century Films and was president of the combined 20th Century Fox from 1942 to 62.[3] The Skouras brothers were so insistent and on hand in Chicago during design and construction of the Ambassador that the Rapps out of self-defense had to give them an office.

Rapp & Rapp's eccentric 1921 version of the Corn Palace exhibition pavilion also arrived unexpectedly when three officials from Mitchell, South Dakota, knocked at the office door after closing time. George Rapp met with the group and sold a plan featuring corn-stalk ornament as a Midwest variation on the leafy swags of high Beaux-Arts they most often provided. Even Italian tenor Tito Schippa, heir to the fame of Enrico Caruso, dropped in with a formal letter introducing himself as Benito Mussolini's government representative, ready to discuss a possible new La Scala opera house in Milan. George spoke no Italian and Schippa little English but they managed.

Along with John Eberson and Thomas Lamb, theatre historians place C.W. & Geo. L. Rapp high on the short list of great American theatre architectural firms. The Rapps were "the Michelangelos of the movie palace," according to Chicago Tribune architecture critic Blair Kamin in an article written in the 1990s, years after the Rapp office had closed. The stunning success of Rapp & Rapp was based on a convenient marriage of skill and the luck of history. Movies came along and the Rapps were ready for them.

When the firm opened in 1907, movies were new technology not ready for respectable theatres. Early films were treated as sideshows, relegated to raffish arcades and long deep storefronts known in

George Leslie Rapp in the 1920s. He was his elder brother's partner in the Chicago firm of C. W. & Geo. L. Rapp, Architects. Because he was the youngest of her nine children, Isaac's wife Georgeina forever called him "Babe." (University of Illinois Archives)

Cornelius Ward Rapp in a formal photograph taken in 1911 at J. Ellsworth Gross studio in Chicago. C. W. Rapp was the guiding force at Chicago's Rapp & Rapp from the firm's beginning in 1907. (Rapp Collection)

the trade as shooting galleries. More respectable popular theatre entertainment consisted of live plays and traveling vaudeville acts, presented in venues owned by show companies like B.F. Keith, Publix, Shubert and the Orpheum circuit.

By 1907 senior partner Cornelius Ward Rapp (1860–1926) already was an established architect, while youngest brother George, an 1899 graduate of the University of Illinois school of architecture, had worked in the office of Chicago architect Edmund C. Krause as draftsman and designer on Chicago's Majestic vaudeville theatre. The Majestic's name later changed to Shubert and presently is Bank of America Theatre. From Krause's Majestic of 1904–06 George with his elder brother took a logical step to neighborhood Chicago vaudeville and nickelodeon houses built by the new firm of C. W. & Geo. L. Rapp. The Rapps' first large theatre job was another named Majestic, built in 1910 in Dubuque, Iowa, now called the Five Flags.

Both born and raised in Carbondale, George Leslie Rapp was C. W.'s junior by eighteen years, an age gap that made a difference. All the Rapp brothers attended Carbondale's normal college, now Southern Illinois University, but only George as the youngest became a graduate architect and fraternity man. This made George's experience more modern. He occupied Rapp & Rapp's front office

The Rapps at a 1902 family reunion in Las Vegas, New Mexico, where William Mason Rapp lived and I. H. & W. M. Rapp had an office. Pictured among the family are all the Rapp architects except Will Rapp's son Mason who wasn't born until 1906 in Trinidad, Colorado. Left to right in the back row are Louis Rapp's wife Martha, C. W. Rapp, W. M. Rapp, Annie Rapp's second husband Frank Clements, and Isaac Hamilton Rapp. In the front row are George L. Rapp, Harriet Rapp Brush, Annie Rapp Bullock Clements, Georgeina and Isaac Rapp, and Louis Rapp. At front are Annie's son E. C. A. "Ted" Bullock and Harriet's son Daniel H. Brush III. Isaac is holding Lou and Martha's son Louie. Harriet's husband D. H. Brush II, a career army officer was serving in the Philippines. Missing too is Trinidad banker Charles R. Rapp. (Rapp Collection)

where he combined natural charm with his talents as architect, salesman, negotiator, idea man and general liaison between clients and staff alike. Privately he gave his job description as "peeing post." One sales tool was his golfing membership in the south suburban Flossmoor Country Club. The club was organized by a group of south side Chicago businessmen, and as the resident architect George was called on periodically to design clubhouse alterations. He never billed the club and they never offered to pay.

When Rapp & Rapp opened, senior partner Cornelius Ward at age 47 had long experience in downstate municipal architecture, in Chicago with Holabird & Roche (later Holabird & Root), and as partner in a Chicago firm named Thomas & Rapp. From 1892 to 97 during the single term of Governor John Peter Altgeld, Rapp took on extra duties as Illinois state architect with an office in Chicago's State of Illinois Building. The Prussian-born Altgeld was the first Democrat governor of Illinois since the Civil War. Most famous and unpopular with the press and much of the public for pardoning three imprisoned Haymarket labor anarchists at the prodding of celebrity lawyer

Clarence Darrow[4], Altgeld created buildings for northern, eastern and southern Illinois college campuses These projects faltered under their first architect whom Altgeld replaced with Rapp, known best at the time for his neoclassical courthouses.

The Rapp buildings for these college campuses were designed in a Collegiate Gothic style with characteristic turrets, battlement crenellations and parapets. Gothic presented a scholarly seriousness common in the design of late 19th century university buildings. Some say the castle design was Altgeld's idea or the concept of the first architect.[5] However this was, Altgeld approved it and C. W. Rapp saw it through at the southern and northern campuses, finishing the "Old Main" building at Eastern Illinois University in Charleston in 1897. A year later he completed the neoclassical Coles County Court House in Charleston. Rapp contributed still another building to the Carbondale campus in 1903—the Romanesque Wheeler Library influenced by the late 19th century style developed by architect Henry Hobson Richardson.[6] Rapp still liked the spirit of the style in 1919 when with his brother George he built the Peoples Theatre in Chicago.

C. W.'s first partnership Thomas & Rapp found itself in accord with the gilded 1890s by designing high-priced Chicago homes, at least one of which remains from 1894 at 1435 N. Astor. Added to in 1902 by architect Henry Ives Cobb, known for his Gothic plan of the University of Chicago, the 20 bedroom gray stone mansion was restored in the early 21st century and placed on the market in 2003 for $22 million, a Chicago real estate listing record according to agents Rubloff Residential Properties.

C. W. Rapp traveled to Japan for six months in 1905, stopping on the way back in Trinidad, Colorado, to visit his brothers who operated under the professional name of I. H. and W. M. Rapp, Architects & Superintendents of Public Buildings. Next he was back in Carbondale helping his aging father Isaac—a contractor, architect, superintendent and planing mill owner but always a carpenter at heart—on Isaac's 1906 Scottish-style First Presbyterian Church. The year 1906 was pivotal for the Rapps in that the church was Isaac's last professional work and C. W. Rapp's final job in southern Illinois, finished only months before he and his youngest brother opened C. W & Geo. L. Rapp in Chicago at 1005 Title & Trust Building, 69 W. Washington. 1906 was also the year Isaac Rapp's fourth son William Mason Rapp in Colorado became father to Mason Gerardi Rapp, the last in the family's unbroken line of architects.

The Gothic Revival Altgeld Hall at Southern Illinois University, Carbondale. The structure combines an elegant castellated Gothic in brick with High Victorian Gothic. As Illinois state architect in the 1890s Cornelius Ward Rapp built this one and two others in similar Collegiate Gothic; Eastern Illinois University at Charleston and Northern Illinois University, Dekalb. (Southern Illinois University)

Carbondale's landmark First Presbyterian Church, designed by C. W. Rapp and built by his father, is known for its authentic use of local limestone and Isaac Rapp's impressive interior vaulted millwork. Still able-bodied at 76, Isaac nevertheless felt the aches and pains of his strenuous life. He kept his "Receipt for Liniment" tacked to the underside of his tool chest lid. Written in pencil and mostly illegible today, the recipe specifies mustard and turpentine among its other long lost ingredients. Isaac lived to be 83 and in his last years was known as Carbondale's oldest citizen. He died two days after Christmas, 1913. During the previous summer a brick parsonage was added to his First Presbyterian Church. Architect for the job was Ted Bullock, son of Isaac's daughter Annie Rapp Bullock Clements. Excepting the Presbyterian Church, little of Isaac Rapp's work stands today. Though his school and university buildings, commercial structures, hotels and residences (including his own house) have given way to changing times, his work ethic lived on through his architect sons.

Cornelius Ward Rapp was Isaac's third son, an able and sober man with innate business sense and high architectural standards. One Rapp & Rapp designer from the 1920s named Theron Woolson summed up C. W. as "that crusty old genius," and chief designer Arthur F. Adams said of his severe appearance that "he always looked sore but he wasn't." To his young designers and draftsmen, who saw him once a day at 11:00 a.m. when he came down the spiral staircase from his office to the drafting room, he was god. He would pass among the broad drafting tables puffing a pipe as he inspected work in progress. Most often he said nothing. Even with his silence, or maybe because of it, no one doubted his authority. Despite his seriousness he was given to expressions of dry humor, such as his observation on the hazards of childhood that "a grown man is an act of God." He never wasted words. To anyone casually asking for free decorating tips his abrupt advice was, "Start with the floor."

C. W. had his own personal rules of order. Whenever he traveled he carried two suitcases, claiming they balanced him. He kept seven ivory-handled straight razors, one for each day of the week, and he wore the boiled collars, monogrammed linen and heavy vested suits stylish in those days. His workdays were long and stressful but he relaxed with a fast walk at noon across Chicago's Loop for lunch and a Havana cigar at his Mid-Day Club. After lunch he withdrew to the billiard room where he lay back on a hard leather couch to close his eyes, holding a cue ball in one hand. On the edge

Isaac Rapp working on a bed frame after his architect son C. W. Rapp helped him finish the First Presbyterian Church in Carbondale. The white card posted on the under-lid of his tool chest is his personal recipe for liniment written in pencil. Turpentine and mustard are the only two ingredients still readable. (Rapp Collection)

First Presbyterian Church, Carbondale, Illinois, as it looked in 1906 when it was completed by Isaac Rapp and his architect son Cornelius Ward Rapp. Built by Isaac Rapp as his last work, the church was designed by C. W. the year before he opened Rapp & Rapp in Chicago with his brother George. 1906 also was the year Isaac's fourth son William Mason Rapp in Trinidad, Colorado, had a son named Mason who became the last in an unbroken line of Rapp family architects. (First Presbyterian Church, Carbondale)

Interior vaulting milled and constructed by Isaac Rapp for Carbondale's First Presbyterian Church, 1906. (Barbara Bennett photo)

In his old age in Carbondale Isaac Rapp was asked if he ever regretted not going to Chicago to rebuild after the disastrous fire of 1871. "No," he replied, "I've always had enough here."[7] But he did have a brother in Chicago named John about whom nothing is known. In his eighties Isaac was known as Carbondale's oldest citizen. (Rapp Collection)

Isaac Rapp's handwriting on an envelope mailed to his son Cornelius Ward Rapp. (Rapp Collection)

Isaac Rapp's signature in 1912. (Rapp Collection)

of sleep when the ball rolled from his hand and hit the floor, he popped awake, considered himself rested and went back to work.

His wife Mary and he each had one ritual martini cocktail every evening of their lives together, even through Prohibition with the service of carriage-trade bootleggers. He prepared the drinks only one way, down to specific brands of liquor: two parts Gordon's gin to one part Martini & Rossi dry vermouth with a drop of orange bitters. He swirled the mixture in a large bed of cold ice, not warm watery cubes which he disdained. If the drinks didn't fill the glasses he poured them back and swirled again until they ran exactly to the rim.

Ward and George Rapp were unalike in character but they worked well together and George depended on his elder brother's knowledge and experience. The relationship between these partners set a working tone for the office that lasted beyond them and throughout the firm's nearly sixty year history; one that was always collegial and low key. Raised voices, moments of panic or fits of temper hardly were known, and duties seemed to gravitate easily to whomever was closest to any job at hand. Work was shared and initiatives trusted, all in keeping with a remark by Colorado brother William Mason Rapp, who observed of his own architectural practice that "responsibility falls to the man who is on the grounds." Still, the Chicago office was no democracy, and Cornelius Ward Rapp was the top-down guiding force. Nothing cleared the office without his approval and nothing got started without his direction. The early Chicago firm, William Rapp's son Mason recalled, "was all Uncle Ward."

2 | THE MEN ON THE GROUNDS

Many architects, artists and engineers passed through Rapp & Rapp from the beginning in 1907, but the careers of only two members spanned nearly the whole history of the firm. Daniel Harmon Brush, III, and Charles A. McCarthy each signed-on not long after the 1909–10 Dubuque Majestic Theatre, took a break in 1917–18 for service in World War I, became partners in the firm in 1940 and worked into the 1960s. The saying goes that no one is indispensable but these two came as close as anyone can; Mac as chief draftsman and Dan as a supervising architect and engineer.

D. H. Brush, III, was born in Carbondale, Illinois, in 1885, the son of Ward and George Rapp's elder sister Harriet Rapp Brush. He always referred to himself as D.H. Brush, Junior, because he thought "the third" sounded too royal and highfalutin. Graduated from the University of Illinois in 1906 as a civil engineer, he went to work for Michigan Gas & Electric and later laid pipe in Chicago's south Loop for Peoples Gas before joining his uncles' firm of Rapp & Rapp. The tough-minded Brush, a thin man whose loosely-fitting suits gave him a rumpled look, always seemed to be lighting his pipe with a billowing flame or fiddling with whatever encrusted one he happened to take from a rack atop one of his two green file cabinets. These metal cabinets, overstuffed with folders, were the only meaningful furniture in his office aside from his desk and two fan-backed wooden chairs. His creaking spring-loaded swivel desk chair allowed him to lean back and prop his feet on the desk while he talked on the phone.

From this sparse office Brush was Rapp & Rapp's expediter; watching over contracts, initialing job specifications, signing change orders and moving the pace of work along by phone, letters and job-site supervision. He knew every contractor and supplier that mattered. His often gruff manner

Daniel Harmon Brush, III, in his 1906 University of Illinois graduation picture. Son of C. W. and George Rapp's sister Harriet who married D. H. Brush, II. Dan joined Rapp & Rapp in Chicago only a few years after the firm opened in 1907. (University of Illinois Archives)

Dan Brush in the 1940s. His half-century career at Rapp & Rapp spanned nearly the whole history of the firm, from the earliest vaudeville and movie houses to high-tech structures of the 1960s. (Brush Collection)

Daniel Harmon Brush, I, the main founder of Carbondale. Illinois, who hired the carpenters Isaac Rapp and James Edwards in 1856 to build his stately home. His grandson D. H. "Dan" Brush III joined the Chicago firm of C. W & Geo. L. Rapp early in his working life, became a full partner in 1940 and remained there until his death twenty years later. (The Lakeside Press)

Georgeina Augusta Shire Rapp, Issac's wife and mother of his nine children. Born at St. Helier on the English Isle of Jersey in 1833, she married Isaac in New York and came to Carbondale with him and their two eldest children in 1855. (Rapp Collection)

Isaac Rapp, father of four architect sons and grandfather of three more. He was born in Orange, New Jersey in 1830. As a carpenter, architect, superintendent and owner of a lumber planing mill in Carbondale, he taught his sons everything he knew. (Rapp Collection)

Isaac and Georgeina Rapp in front of the home Isaac built for his family at 406 W. Main Street, Carbondale. Their daughter Annie Rapp Clements lived there until her death in 1946. The home was razed in 1950. (Rapp Collection)

worked on job sites, but could seem brusque to clients. Often he appeared preoccupied, and at home liked to do woodwork alone in his basement or tend his garden roses. Socially he had an amiable, even courtly manner. It was usual for men of those days not to talk of work at home. Dan Brush was no exception.

His grandfather Daniel Harmon Brush, I, was the son of one Elkanah Brush, a leathery Vermont pioneer with a keen survival instinct who rafted down the Ohio River to southern Illinois in the 1830s. Elkanah's son D.H. became founding father of the city of Carbondale, Illinois, was a strict abolitionist, a Lincoln Republican, a bearded Presbyterian of the old school and a teetotaler so strict on himself and others that he wrote "no liquor" clauses into business contracts which would nullify the documents if any signatory ever took a drink.

George and C.W. Rapp's father Isaac, four of whose nine children would become architects, got to know D.H. Brush, I, when as a young carpenter he built Brush's large home in 1856–57 with partner James Edwards. Edwards had worked in a lumber mill owned by Brush, and with the promise of a business partnership in 1855 he lured the 25-year-old Isaac Rapp to southern Illinois from New York City where the two had been cabinetmakers together. With the Illinois Central Railroad charter line about to reach completion in 1856 (with Brush's influence on routing the rails through Carbondale), Isaac Rapp saw promise in southern Illinois and left New York with his wife Georgeina and two small children, Harriet and Isaac Hamilton Rapp.

Edwards & Rapp got the job for the Brush home based on bids. According to Brush the young carpenters underestimated their time and materials by a long way. When the job was finished Edwards & Rapp stood by their original quotes, but Brush had them recalculate their costs and paid them a fair price. The Brush home is long gone but a tantalizing word picture appears in the introduction to Brush's published memoir titled Growing Up With Southern Illinois:

"The entire place was enclosed by a thick hedge, within which magnolias, cape jasmines, and numerous other trees flourished, while flower beds, stables, a greenhouse, a fishpond, and other appurtenances suitable to a prosperous estate were ranged in orderly array."[1]

The abstract concepts of architecture are translated to the real world in two basic ways: design and drafting. Designers provide a building's outward appearance while draftsmen draw the floor plans and internal structure. Charles A. "Mac" McCarthy was a master of the second category.

A second generation Irish-American from Chicago's south side; Mac served in WWI as a signalman on the bridge of the battleship Pennsylvania. His father drove a horse-drawn streetcar for a living and had been a young soldier in the Civil War. Mac in the 1950s casually wore the old man's Union field jacket while he wet-sanded his boat. A lifelong bachelor, Olympic figure skater and latter-day yachtsman who started at Rapp & Rapp as a plan boy, McCarthy became a licensed architect by determination and many hours of night school at Armour Institute on Chicago's south side. Armour later became Illinois Institute of Technology, today a living museum of buildings designed in the 1950s by IIT's guiding spirit Ludwig Mies van der Rohe, where the motto among some of his architecture students became "glass and steel, that's the deal."

Charles A. McCarthy (left), Rapp & Rapp's chief draftsman, joined the office not long after Dan Brush. More than one McCarthy associate thought him a rare genius, but the low-key McCarthy never seemed impressed with himself or the camera, which explains why this snapshot contains his only remaining likeness. Taken in July, 1961, Mac is in Rapp & Rapp's Michigan Avenue office working on the Fisher Theatre with draftsman Franz Weber. To keep his neckwear out of his work McCarthy always wore bow ties. (Rapp Collection)

When Mac went to night school he worked at Rapp & Rapp by day. One afternoon George Rapp needed quick changes on plans for a client waiting in the front office. Rapp asked around for a draftsman but it was late and all had gone. The plan boy McCarthy, still sweeping up the day's pencil shavings, quietly offered to do the job. Rapp raised his eyebrows but let Mac try. McCarthy produced changes that were expert in every way. The amazed George Rapp promoted him on the spot from plan boy to draftsman.

McCarthy was a tireless workman who hunched over his large table for hours on end, moving his triangle and T square so quickly they seemed part of his hands. No one ever thought of coffee breaks at Rapp & Rapp (or health care benefits, pensions, air-conditioning, anything less than a five and a half day week or for that matter social security which, even when it was legislated, did not cover architects), but to refresh himself Mac would stand from his swivel stool and pursing his lips stare blankly out the window or amble from office to office for short chats, his glasses in hand and rubbing his eyes.

When a new job came to the office Mac was first to get the plat of survey along with preliminary specifications. Typically he withdrew to a corner table to make mysterious marks and tics on tiny scraps of paper. Today Revit and CAD 3-D computer systems would do his job, but with these paper scraps and his spatial sense Mac determined from every angle the most efficient way to site a structure and maximize theatre seating (seating equates to money). Within hours he would produce preliminary plans for each building level, essentially presenting a working point of departure

Arthur Adams (center, in derby hat) living the picturesque bistro life in 1912 Paris during his time at Ecole de Beaux Arts. (Adams Collection)

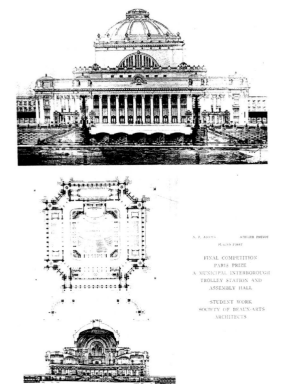

Arthur F. Adams in the late 1920s when he was chief designer for Rapp & Rapp. A Paris Prize winner at Ecole de Beaux Arts, he joined the Chicago firm in 1921 just as the movie palace industry was expanding across the country. (Adams Collection)

Adams' Paris Prize-winning work developed according to the required Beaux Arts method showing elevation (front view), section (side view) and floor plan. (Adams Collection) for the course of the job. Robert K. Bauerle, an architect with Rapp & Rapp in the 1940s, recalled McCarthy as a genius, while Arthur Frederick Adams, the Rapps' chief designer in the 20s and 30s, remembered Mac as "the best in the country." Mason Rapp carried the compliment further when he recalled Adams himself as simply "the best."

Architect Arthur F. Adams (1883–1977) was a third Rapp & Rapp indispensable who came to the office later than Brush and McCarthy and left earlier but whose design work helped cover the Rapp theatres in glory through the 1920s. The unprecedented elegance and sheer size of Chicago's Tivoli Theatre, opened just after Valentine's Day in 1921, meant that Rapp & Rapp, movie studios and theatre operators across the country had seen their future.

With the downtown Chicago Theatre set to open the following October, the Rapps needed someone to head the design department. The new man would have to handle big, spectacular jobs quickly and expertly. Office designer A. S. "Bumps" Graven knew Adams through mutual connections and introduced him as a candidate. A Paris Prize design winner at École des Beaux-Arts, Adams started with the office just before the October 1921 Chicago Theatre opening at a generous annual salary for the time of $10,000.

Among his early assignments with the office was a trip to Cleveland with draftsman Guy Mayger to assess work on the B. F. Kieth theatre and office building. During the trip Mayger tried to interest Adams in leaving Rapp & Rapp to join him in the dream of a new partnership. Having just joined Rapp & Rapp, Adams rejected Mayger's offer. Besides facing an obvious ethical problem, Adams realized the Rapps knew key industry people and had wide business connections while Mayger did not. It turned out that Mayger and designer Graven did leave Rapp & Rapp to form their own firm. Good architects though they were, Graven & Mayger never matched the output of Rapp & Rapp. Adams was right; the Rapps knew the people and had the connections.

Born in London where his father was a writer, brought up in Spokane and naturalized as an American citizen in 1905, Adams attended Columbia University and Pratt Institute before winning rigorous design competitions that sent him to Paris and the École des Beaux-Arts. In those days every major architectural school in the western world taught the profession by the Beaux-Arts method, and all the world of art, architecture and design had to check a natural reflex to bow before anyone holding a Paris medal, civilization's badge of honor and standard of excellence back to King Louis XIV.

Adams arrived at Rapp & Rapp as something of a romantic curiosity to the mostly midwestern fraternity boys who staffed the drafting and design departments; more than 150 of them in the peak years. Most were very young, underpaid and given to eraser throwing and tasteless jokes. Over the years many left Rapp & Rapp for more pay and dreams of greater promise, but after a time doing Chicago bungalows and the like most came back for the adventure of theatre design. In his Paris Beaux-Arts days Adams attended artist's balls and lived the good life in the City of Lights that would attract American expatriates in the 1920s. To the young design boys at Rapp & Rapp, Adams seemed suspiciously sophisticated with his full cravats, slouchy fedoras and longer hair than the close-cut staff around him.

Adams was an architect with talents beyond creative design at Rapp & Rapp, including job supervision, business planning and publicity. Informally he assumed the task of in-house historian, saving sketches, photographs, press releases which he wrote himself, and news clippings preserved in a series of his personal scrapbooks. These were real contribution since the Rapps seemed unmindful of recording for posterity beyond the buildings themselves. For the National Terra Cotta Society, Adams took a summer tour of Italy in 1923 to take photographs for a 1925 book called *Terra Cotta of the Italian Renaissance*. The Society's idea was to promote the use of sculpted terra cotta (fired clay) as a durable and decorative cladding for modern buildings. Before the 1920s, when it became widely used by architects including Rapp & Rapp in theatre facades and office building exteriors, the virtues of terra cotta mostly had been ignored since the Renaissance. The Renaissance masters of glazed polychrome terra cotta were the Robbia family; Andrea, Giovanni, Luca and Dei della Robia. Adams photos concentrated heavily on their work. That the della Robbias' legacy had stood the test of time, weather and Italy's sunlight seemed advertisement enough for the Terra Cotta Society.

While at Rapp & Rapp Adams submitted a scheme for the Chicago Tribune Tower design competition in 1922, an architectural event so major that it attracted world entries. The judges termed Adams' submission "the most American" among the entries, which took a first honorable mention behind Finnish architect Eero Saarinen, Chicago's Holabird & Roche and the ultimate winner Raymond M. Hood of Howells & Hood. Adams finally did win a Tribune competition in 1945 for WGN (World's Greatest Newspaper) radio station's Theatre of the Air building. The structure was to have abutted Howells & Hood's original tower. Adams collected his $5,000 prize money but the building for WGN never went ahead; a victim of coming television.

Adams, with this 1922 Tribune Tower submission, took a First Honorable Mention behind winner Raymond Hood, second place Eero Saarinen, and third place Holabird & Roche. (Adams Collection)

At the time of the 1922 Tribune competition, Rapp designer Theron Woolson had prepared an entry of his own. Woolson had worked for Burnham & Root before coming to Rapp & Rapp through McCarthy. The Tribune Tower entry he so laboriously prepared (carefully cleaning the surface with loaves of bread—a usual practice) was ineligible because Woolson was not a licensed (state approved) architect; but his friend McCarthy was. He asked Mac to let him use his name. Mac, who never did design work and never explained why, agreed and Woolson's entry was accepted, finishing back in the pack under the name of Charles A. McCarthy.

Throughout the 1920s Adams organized and attended so-called "ateliers" for Chicago designers. Like ancient guilds these select groups compared notes, gossiped, staged sketch competitions among themselves, taught the less experienced, passed job tips to the unemployed among them and hosted parties with bootlegged liquor in an atmosphere blue with tobacco smoke. They all possessed rare talent and were proud of it, always pushing for the better design, the new way or the more spectacular scheme.

Another key architect in the early office was Edwin Corliss Atlee (Ted) Bullock, born at Fort Riley, Kansas, to C.W. and George Rapp's other sister Annie Augusta Rapp Bullock Clements (1866–1946). Bullock's father Edwin C. Bullock was with George Custer's 7th Cavalry when in the 1870s he was sent to quell an Indian uprising in Arizona. Following on he became a math professor at the University of Wyoming ROTC School in Laramie. He died of pneumonia in 1893 leaving his widow Annie with their four-year-old son Ted. Annie married again, to Frank Clements, a respected Carbondale businessman. As his uncle George Rapp had done before him, Ted got his architecture degree from the University of Illinois, class of 1909. He also followed both George and Dan Brush into Sigma Chi fraternity. Ted Bullock is noteworthy for pushing the idea of a Rapp & Rapp New York office and for heading that office after it opened in 1926. Like Arthur Adams, Bullock wrote publicity pieces and scholarly and technical essays for professional journals.[2]

Bullock married three times. His first wife was killed during World War I driving a rough dirt road to a Red Cross meeting in Defiance, Ohio. When her top-heavy touring car hit a rut and rolled, she struck her head and died instantly. The daughter Anne she had with Ted was one year old. A family friend called "Mama Azu", who was too old to keep the child for long, took Ann in. Ted's second wife died of pneumonia shortly after marriage, leaving Bullock again to care for Anne alone. He returned to Carbondale, left Anne with his mother Annie and Frank Clements, and headed for Chicago to work for Rapp & Rapp. Ted regularly sent

The second nephew to work in Chicago for Rapp & Rapp was Edwin C. A. "Ted" Bullock, son of C. W. and George's sister Annie Rapp Bullock Clements. In 1912 Ted built an addition to the Carbondale First Presbyterian Church his grandfather Isaac and uncle C. W. Rapp built in 1906. A University of Illinois graduate architect like his Uncle George, Ted headed Rapp & Rapp's New York office, opened in the early 1920s to supervise construction on the Paramount building and theatre at Times Square. He liked New York so much he stayed-on after George closed the branch office. (University of Illinois Archives)

money for Anne's care, as Annie and Frank Clements became the girl's de facto parents. Anne always referred to her grandmother as "Momsy."

To cut costs Ted took a room in George Rapp's double apartment in the Windermere West, an old-line Victorian mainly residential hotel near the Museum of Science and Industry and the University of Chicago in the Hyde Park neighborhood. C. W. Rapp had an apartment there as well during the early Rapp & Rapp years, though after marriage in 1911 Mary and he moved into a larger apartment in a Blackstone Avenue court building. Ted moved permanently to New York in 1926 and married his third wife Rita. His former space in George Rapp's apartment was always referred to as "Ted's room", even as it devolved into a storage area for piles of oriental rugs, lamps and odd pieces of furniture.

Without one other member of the firm the office might have failed its mission. Veronica Walsh was no architect, designer or draftsman but she was an expert administrator. As George Rapp's secretary she ran the Rapp & Rapp's daily operation. Like an untitled CEO she oversaw personnel and payroll, gave order to the vast quantities of paperwork every job produced, coordinated appointments and meetings, handled correspondence and clients with equal skill and generally kept chaos at bay. Her dedication was complete, her hours were long, and her salary was rich.

The Rapp & Rapp enterprise during the 1920s was a crucible for several architects and designers who successfully moved on and became well known on their own. A. S. Graven and Guy Mayger formed their Chicago partnership in 1927, Temple Buell went on to Denver for a long career and S. Charles Lee left to practice theatre architecture in California. The strange and obsessive Louis Bourgeois left Rapp & Rapp to spend years designing and building the world center of the Bahai faith, the looming Bahai Temple at the lake front in Wilmette north of Chicago.

3 | RISK AND REWARD

Through the 1920s, movie palaces became certain money makers for independent exhibitors and major studios alike, but it was not so in the beginning when caution was the wise man's friend. Among the most visionary entrepreneurs and merchandisers in this uncertain time were the Balaban family (Abe, John, Barney, Max, David, Harry, Elmer and sister Ida) and their partner Sam Katz, who had operated successful nickelodeon theatres on his own. Before they got into theatres, the Russian Jewish immigrant Balabans ran a grocery store near the open markets and stalls of Maxwell Street, Chicago's center of streetwise capitalism.[1] They began to like the idea that theatre patrons paid for the product in advance. There were no running tabs, accounts receivable or bill collections. All was clear profit, up front. Still, there were the risks of the unknown, and Balaban & Katz, eventually Rapp & Rapp's prime clients, moved carefully at the outset of a young movie industry with a vague future.

The questions were many. Who would come to see movies? Could shadowy flickering silent images projected onto a screen compete with the excitement of live vaudeville? What sort of venue would movie patrons welcome and where should these places be located? Would there be enough patrons to make a difference, and if a small house was good would a big house that's more expensive to operate be better? All these and other questions needed practical answers for which there were no guide books.

In the earliest days, nickelodeon movie houses were socially suspect; entertaining but somehow not respectable. This attitude prevailed when in 1907 the Balabans first rented the Kedzie Theatre, where Abe Balaban had been a part time singer with an eye for greater possibilities. Coincidentally 1907 was the year Rapp & Rapp designed its first theatre, the San Souci nickelodeon located in the White City amusement park, which had opened two years previously at 63rd Street and South Park

The nickelodeon San Souci, Rapp & Rapp's first theatre design, was built in 1907 on the grounds of the White City amusement park, 63rd and South Park, Chicago. The site was on the former midway of the 1893 Chicago World's Fair. (Chicago History Museum)

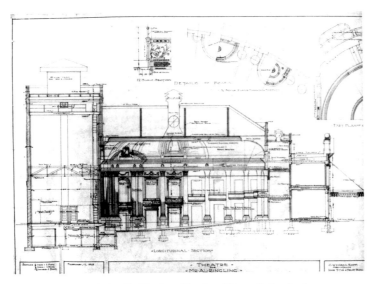

Sectional detail of the Al. Ringling Theatre. (Rapp Collection)

Al. Ringling interior.
(Rapp Collection)

on the former midway of the 1893 Columbian Exposition. With the Kedzie the Balabans realized the need for quality production, theatre cleanliness and customer comfort, all characteristic of B&K's ultimate 125-theatre Midwest empire. Using street barkers and lively recorded music piped to the outside, the Kedzie was a quick triumph. This gave the Balabans confidence enough to borrow money for the nearby Circle Theatre, which they opened in 1909. In addition to movies, it featured a small house orchestra, pipe organ and name acts booked by Abe Balaban, which elevated the Circle above its nickelodeon competition.

Rapp & Rapp followed San Souci with Chicago's Bryn Mawr (1908) and a larger theatre in Dubuque, Iowa, called the Majestic (1910). Following-on were the Racine, Wisconsin, Orpheum (1912), and Chicago's Windsor (1913) built on the long narrow site at 1235 N. Clark Street, where a first Windsor had been destroyed by fire. After that came the La Salle Theatre at 152 W. Division, and the downstate Illinois Orpheums in Champaign and Quincy, all opened in 1914. Along with the Rockford Palace in 1915 came the crowning achievement among these early examples, the glistening Al. Ringling Theatre in Baraboo, Wisconsin. That

The Palace of Versailles Chapel frequently was used by Rapp & Rapp as a model for movie palace lobbies, with a grand staircase replacing the altar at the end. The design, modified to handle large crowds, never failed to impress incoming theatre patrons. (Editions d'Art Lys)

near perfect job was commissioned by Al. Ringling, the eldest of seven Ringling brothers, as a gift to the town that was headquarters for the circus that bore his family name. Chicago's Central Park Theatre, built by Rapp & Rapp for Balaban & Katz in 1917, was a blend of characteristics developed in the Windsor and Ringling.

The earliest Rapp theatres typically featured mezzanine box seating, stage boxes, and sidewalls with simple trellis or latticework treatments. The move from painted Victorian treillage toward Rapp & Rapp's signature Versailles and Second Empire elegance took root in just one year between the Racine Orpheum of 1912 and the 1913 Windsor Theatre, after C. W. Rapp saw Paris first hand. The Windsor's layout began to suggest the golden age of Versailles with influences brought to realization in the Ringling two years later. The Champaign Orpheum of 1914 amounted to a replica of Versailles' La Salle de Spectacle at a third of the size, and was constructed solidly enough to last as long—the Rapps built for keeps, typically using an excess of steel and concrete. The Windsor, Champaign Orpheum and Ringling designs were, like many things with Rapp & Rapp, born of timely happenstance recognized by ready minds. One of these timely events occurred in 1911 when

Entertainments Room at the Palace of Versailles. Everything about this room influenced C. W. Rapp when he saw it in 1912. Rapp & Rapp transformed this Louis XV style into the signature elegance of their 20th century movie palaces. (Editions d'Art Lys)

2042. - SCÈNES et TYPES - Gourbis dans le Sud - E. S.

During the 1911–12 wedding trip to Europe and north Africa Mary P. R. Rapp regularly sent exotic post cards like this one to her husband's brother Will's children, Mason and Mary Georgeina in Trinidad, Colorado. (Rapp Collection)

C.W. Rapp at age 51 married the twenty years younger Mary Payne Root and sailed off on a wedding trip to Europe and north Africa. In those days overseas travel was a major commitment—all ships and steamer trunks. During the six month trip Mary regularly sent picture postcards to her husband's brother Will's little son and daughter Mason and Mary G. at home in Colorado.

Stepdaughter of a railroad executive, Mary had early access to free rail travel which before her marriage she used adventurously, touring many American wildernesses before they became national parks. She loved the outdoors and liked to invite guests on camping retreats complete with horses, pack mules and tents near Taos, New Mexico, where, she said, it rained every afternoon at three o'clock. Mary became a world traveler as well, mailing picture post cards of monumental architecture to C.W. in Chicago from Rome, Paris, London and Cologne, whose great cathedral she reported as "a good bunch of gothic well worth seeing." Often from her home in Red Bluff, California, where her mother founded the local Episcopal Church, she had visited family in Quincy, Illinois, where she may have met C.W. Rapp as he traveled on business. No one knows how or when they were introduced but their small remaining correspondence suggests they knew each other before there was a Rapp & Rapp, at least as early as 1905. By 1911, the year of their marriage, Mary was convinced Europe would benefit her husband's work.

On their way the couple stopped in Moylen, Pennsylvania, where Rapp met members of his new wife's family. During dinner the maid filled table glasses from a pitcher containing water poured over the last of the martini cocktails. As told by Mary P. R. Rapp, her husband tasted the gin flavored water and whispered to his hostess, "I admire your well."

During the couple's long honeymoon George Rapp ran the office in Chicago and guided progress on Rapp & Rapp's biggest job since the 1910 Dubuque Majestic, the 570-seat Orpheum in Racine. The Rapps employed a local man named J. D. Hogan as job superintendent. Hiring local superintendents was common in the days when travel was time-consuming. During the busiest years Rapp & Rapp was able to handle numerous jobs simultaneously around the country by employing people like Hogan. These superintending "clerks of the works," as they were named, usually were local architects, highly skilled, honored to be chosen and not underpaid. They supervised day-to-day construction as architect's agent but could not authorize change orders and were limited to routine decisions. C.W. and George Rapp's father Isaac himself had worked as builder and superintendent for an outside architect on Southern Illinois University's Old Main building of 1877. Besides clerks and superintendents there were always general contractors, often called builders, to rely on between visits by architects from the office.

The Racine Orpheum was equipped with a projection booth, but in 1912 movies were still upstaged in public taste by vaudeville acts (quick-change artists, monologists, posing dogs and the like) booked by large, experienced and entrenched agencies. A local reporter at the Orpheum opening wrote only that "the moving pictures are clear and of the very latest that the films can produce." Although C.W. had not yet brought the full glory of France back with him, the quiet elegance of the Orpheum received the sort of gushing press coverage to which the Rapp office became accustomed. The Racine Journal-News of April 30, 1912 wrote of opening night:

"Descriptions of the place have not been exaggerated... Reaching the lobby, expressions of surprise were heard, still more was this surprise in evidence when the foyer was reached, both elaborately decorated and luxuriously furnished. But it was in the body of the house that the astonishment broke loose. No one had anticipated anything nearly as beautiful... thirteen mezzanine boxes directly to the east and over the rear of the auditorium proper, finished in ivory and decorations of old rose."

The seats were "roomy and comfortable, concrete floors covered with carpets, delicately tinted ceilings" and chandeliers with forty lights, an impressive number at the time but a paltry glitter compared with the Victor Pearlman chandeliers, grand dome cove lighting and marquee chasers of the coming movie palaces. The Racine paper pointed out that balcony seating was "so raised and arranged that every seat gives a clear view of the stage and performers," revealing C.W. Rapp's early and ongoing obsession with theatre sight lines, or what he called "eye command." He devised improved sight lines by working out main floor pitch formulas with back-of-the-envelope calculations, all according to number of seats and floor square-footage. A matter of inches in slope made the difference between viewing the stage comfortably and having to dodge the patron's head in front. The floor-pitch numbers were extrapolated for drafting room use into sets of wooden rules and templates custom-made for the office by the tool company Keuffel & Esser. Though proprietary, Rapp's pitch formulas eventually were pirated and began to appear recognizably in the work of other theatre architects. Soon the calculations became industry commonplace, appearing even now in Graphics & Standards publications.

C.W. Rapp was due to return from Europe in time for the Racine Orpheum's April opening. Mary and he had booked passage on the maiden voyage of the White Star Line's RMS Titanic scheduled for an early April sailing from Southampton, England, to New York. Meanwhile the couple took in the limitless aspects of the Chateau de Versailles with its drawing rooms named for the deities of ancient Greece; its apartments, chambers and antechambers; its halls and libraries; Louis XV's Entertainments Room with its intimate feel and sunburst proscenium arch, along with the soaring, columned Chapel of Versailles which would come to inform the grandest of Rapp & Rapp's grand lobbies.

As the Titanic's sailing date approached it was clear there was more to be seen, and "Wardy," as Mary called him, likely wouldn't get back to France any time soon. There was still Marie Antoinette's Petit Trianon, and Rapp hadn't even begun to exhaust the Second Empire complexities of L'Opera de Paris, a mighty edifice commissioned from architect Charles Garnier by Napoleon III and completed thirty-six years before the Rapps' wedding trip. On Mary's insistence the couple agreed to cancel their Titanic voyage, avoiding the events of April 14, 1912, when the ship struck an iceberg and went down in the north Atlantic. Six years earlier Mary barely avoided the other major disaster of the early 20th century when she left San Francisco by train in April 1906, only hours before the earthquake and fire that consumed the city.

Rapp armed himself with a wealth of on-site information about the shape and feel of classic Beaux-Arts treatment and brought home a trunk of books, most notably two large volumes of Charles Garnier's color renderings of Paris Opera detail, and collections of Piranesi studies of classical Rome. Over time Rapp & Rapp assembled a considerable architectural library whose volumes were stamped and numbered as property of the firm, all locked inside cabinets in George Rapp's office. Designers from Arthur Adams' department regularly pored over the books for motifs and inspiration. Rapp

Cornelius Ward Rapp, 1912, in his Windermere West Hotel apartment. Rapp lived there with his wife Mary after their long wedding trip, during which he absorbed and personalized the architecture of France. (Rapp Collection)

found Europe so basic to his understanding that he urged brother George to go and see for himself, which he did a few years later.

Still on his way back from Paris with his new bride, C. W. missed the grand pre-opening night gala at the Racine Orpheum, April 29, 1912. Theatre management auctioned off for charity the mezzanine box seats, all eagerly bought-up by society patrons. The house brimmed with theatrical people, including the Orpheum circuit's general manager, president of the Western Vaudeville Association, the Allardt circuit managers, the general manager of the Vaudeville Managers Association and many booking agents. Among them was Sam Kahl from the family for whom Rapp & Rapp would build the Kahl Building and Capitol Theatre (1919) in Davenport, Iowa. At evening's end the Racine theatre's manager H.C. Andrees rose to introduce dignitaries. George Rapp was beckoned to the stage to receive what Andrees called "just applause" for an impressive job, but George declined the honor with a wave from his main floor seat.

Theatre executives in attendance were the cream of the vaudeville industry that had yet to give way to movies. Newcomer nickelodeon operators like Sam Katz and the Balabans were not among them. The Racine Orpheum was a creditable job, but it turned out to be Rapp & Rapp's last in a more circumspect Victorian style about to give way to more ornate movie palaces. The office's French conception began with C.W. Rapp's return from Europe, introduced in the 1913 Windsor Theatre, developed with the Champaign and Quincy Orpheums and refined in the Al. Ringling in Baraboo.

The year 1912 brought another change as well; the start of a longstanding distance between Mary P. R. Rapp and George Rapp. George regarded Mary as a meddlesome distraction while Mary disapproved of George's lifestyle, namely that by her standards he drank too much. They rarely saw each other. Mary in fact could seem self-righteous and she believed her place in the family as wife of the senior partner somehow put her ahead of others. She also believed alcohol abuse was a character flaw, and thought it good to serve children a little wine at dinner that they might learn how to partake wisely as adults. She liked to tell small children morality tales and was fond of using her hands to explain the three monkeys "see no evil, speak no evil, hear no evil." She told the story of another monkey that reached into a jar of peanuts and clutched so many he could not remove his fist. Because he would not settle for fewer peanuts he got none at all. She tended to form quick inflexible impressions; if she approved of you all was well, but if she didn't you were silently condemned. The simple power of the old Protestant hymns affected her. Particular favorites were "Shall We Gather at the River" and "Rock of Ages," but her musical tastes were wider than that. She liked Chicago Symphony Orchestra concerts in the University of Chicago's Mandel Hall, and after she saw a performance by the young folk singer Burl Ives she was amazed at how one man with a guitar could hold the audience's rapt attention for three hours.

Mary's primary ambition was to be wife and homemaker. She could have had domestic help at the Rapps large new apartment in the court building at 1428 E. 57th Street, but chose to do all the housework herself. All the decorating choices, cooking, cleaning, washing and ironing she took on enthusiastically. She believed no homemaker should be without a mangle for pressing sheets. Nothing was too much for her to do, and she loved the domestic life.

As for George, he did come to drink too much and was first to admit it. He suffered quietly from a form of epilepsy that produced petit-mal seizures which he claimed alcohol helped control. These unpredictable events momentarily made his face stiffen into an eerie blank and caused his eyelids to flutter. The era was intolerant of such afflictions but George mostly was able to conceal it except from those closest to him.

Personality conflicts aside, there is no denying Mary's part in introducing first hand the architectural glories of France to her husband and into Rapp & Rapp's most recognizable style. The richness of this high Beaux-Arts as Rapp & Rapp developed it was not lost on the Balabans. They knew about the Champaign Orpheum, Windsor and the other early Rapp & Rapps, and Sam Katz was pleased with what he saw when he went to Baraboo for a look at the Al. Ringling. Balaban & Katz hired Rapp & Rapp in 1916 to build north side Chicago's Riviera Theatre and the west side Central Park, which opened first in 1917. World War I shortages delayed the Rivera opening to 1918.

The Central Park at 3535 W. Roosevelt Road was Chicago's first movie palace and probably first in the world, depending on the subtleties of definition. Some historians give the title to Thomas Lamb's 1919 Capitol Theatre in New York, but the Capitol was basically a traditional box built large, a palace only because of its greater size. The smaller but still large Central Park was first to include movie-friendly innovations that no later cinema palace could have done without, including improved sight lines, discrete exit stairways from balcony to grade level and larger lobby spaces to accommodate audiences simultaneously leaving one showing and arriving for the next. This solved a crowd circulation problem that single performance legitimate playhouses never had to consider.

By coincidence Rapp & Rapp's 1921 Chicago Theatre at 175 N. State Street was drawn-up in 1919 as the Capitol, the year Lamb's Capitol opened. Theatre owners often changed their minds about theatre names. As the first movie palace built on choice and expensive downtown property, the Chicago Theatre's impact on the film industry was immediate and explosive.

4 | THE BIG SISTERS

Rapp & Rapp moved the office in 1918 from the Title & Trust Building to the two top floors of the State-Lake Building, 190 N. State Street. The State-Lake was designed by Rapp & Rapp and housed a theatre of the same name designed by west coast architect G. Albert Lansburgh.

Half way through the job, American involvement in World War I siphoned-off domestic steel supplies which threatened the project's completion. Rapp & Rapp solved the problem by using reinforced concrete in place of steel for the building's upper stories. Strengthening concrete with steel rods was not new—C. W. and George's architect brothers I. H. & W. M. Rapp had used the material in the walls of Santa Fe's impenetrable jail—but the State-Lake was an early application, forced by necessity, to high-rise building construction.

The State-Lake's mixed-use of a theatre within a larger building was a selling point that George Rapp often put forward to encourage prospective owner/developers. If a theatre failed, building rents would pay the way and vice versa. Other Rapp & Rapp combinations of this sort included the Kahl Building and Capitol Theatre (1920), Davenport, Iowa; the Bismarck Hotel, Palace Theatre and Metropolitan Office Building (1926), Chicago; the Oriental Theatre and New Masonic Temple Building (1926), Chicago; and the Fox Theatre and National Press Club Building (1926), Washington, D.C. The earliest movie houses were more apt to be free-standing; like the Riviera, the design of which was begun in Rapp & Rapp's Title & Trust office and finished in the new State-Lake location. Another design carried over to the State-Lake from the old office was the Peoples Theatre, opened in 1919 on Chicago's 47th Street. The Peoples was built for H. Schoenstadt & Sons, south side theatre managers who hired Rapp & Rapp again in 1926 for the Piccadilly Theatre and Hotel at Hyde Park Boulevard and Blackstone.

Rapp & Rapp finished Chicago's State-Lake Building in 1918 and moved their offices into the top two floors. (Rapp Collection)

The Kahl Building and Capitol Theatre in Davenport (1920), similar in treatment to the State-Lake project though smaller, was typical of the dual-use theatre/office building combinations Rapp & Rapp sold to clients. (Rapp Collection)

Capitol Theatre stairs within the Kahl Building, Davenport, Iowa. (Rapp Collection)

The Press building's grand niche above the Fox Theatre marquee and vertical sign. Rapp & Rapp used the grand niche only twice, here and in Rubens' Rialto Theatre, Joliet, Illinois. (Arthur Adams, Jr.)

Capitol Theatre, Davenport, opened just a year before the Chicago and Tivoli. (Rapp Collection)

Rapp & Rapp's early 1919 office building/theatre combination for B. F. Keith, Cincinnati.

A romanticized office rendering of the Schoenstadts' Peoples Theatre, 1919. (Rapp Collection)

The Peoples Theatre finished on Chicago's south side in 1919 for H. Schoenstadt & Sons emphasized long sweeping arches derived from the work of Henry Hobson Richardson, a major architectural influence not lost on the Rapps in Chicago or their brother architects in Trinidad, Colorado. (Rapp Collection)

To the Peoples, C. W. Rapp applied Gothic vaulting in the lobby and sweeping Romanesque arches for the auditorium influenced by the work of architect Henry Hobson Richardson. Richardson also influenced C. W. and George's brothers I. H. and W. M. Rapp in their Trinidad, Colorado, school and bank work, as he did many architects of the time. The visual result of the Peoples was sober compared to the French ornamental outbursts that lay just ahead for Rapp & Rapp. In view directly across State Street from the Rapps' new State-Lake headquarters lay the property which two years after the Peoples would become the site of the Chicago Theatre. This 3800-seat giant along with the south side Tivoli started Rapp & Rapp's French revolution.

The Tivoli and Chicago theatres for Balaban & Katz, both on the drafting tables in 1919, were opened to the public in 1921. Often called "sisters", though they were not alike in appearance, these two houses brought trend-setting showmanship to the world of entertainment and moved the Rapps to the head of the class among modern theatre architects. Architect W. W. Alschlager's Senate Theatre, which opened in Chicago in the same year, paled in comparison to the two new Rapp palaces. When he saw the Tivoli, Alschlager, who later designed New York's massive Roxy Theatre, is said to have remarked, "I laid an egg." This admission aside, the Rapp's secretly envied Alschlager's ability to sell his work. Later projects by Rapp & Rapp and every other theatre architect used applications developed in the Tivoli and Chicago as the industry launched into a decade-long movie palace binge.

A third major multiple-use job in the busy year of 1926 was Chicago's Masonic Building and Oriental Theatre. The wary owners insisted that Rapp & Rapp give the building separate structural support in case the theatre failed and had to be torn out. (Chicago History Museum)

The Oriental Theatre, Rapp & Rapp's most fantastic interior, explores the limits of what could be done with drapery and ornament. (Chicago History Museum)

Applications and specifications developed in these two theatres became so common from one job to another that George Rapp and Dan Brush kept near their telephones quick-reference desk copies of loose-leaf notebooks called "Typicals and Standards." These shorthand books included rough costs per seat, kino (projection) booth and stage trap specs, stage nosing and footlight designs, various basic floor plans and other routine items, all of which contributed to patron comfort beyond the obvious visual experience. Rapp & Rapp often borrowed their own designs and motifs from one job to another. The Oriental in Chicago and the St. Louis Ambassador shared proscenium and organ screen design while the dome and mezzanine foyer in the Joliet Rialto and Shea's Buffalo Theatre were almost alike. Similar plan and detail appeared in the Chicago Theatre and Loew's Penn in Pittsburgh and even comparable animal ornament appeared in Chicago's Old Dearborn Bank, Uptown Theatre and the rotunda columns of the Joliet Rialto. There are many examples of this sort of useful cross-referencing.

Much of the success of these earliest movie palaces came from B & K's canny sense for site location. The Tivoli went up at 63rd and Cottage Grove, a south side neighborhood hub of public transportation billed as the city's busiest intersection outside of the Loop, while the Chicago was the nation's first movie palace built on expensive downtown property. Both were big financial risks and the Balabans took on mountains of debt to bring them off. Much seed money came from financier A.W. Strauss whose Chicago offices at 6 N. Clark were remodeled by Rapp & Rapp at the time the Chicago and Tivoli were on the drawing boards. When the two theatres paid for themselves within months everyone in the industry noticed.

Though sisters in time they were not identical twins. The Chicago recalled 19th century France with an Arc de Triomphe front elevation outlined with stud lighting, while the Tivoli's baroque

Front elevation of the Tivoli Theatre, Chicago.
(Rapp Collection)

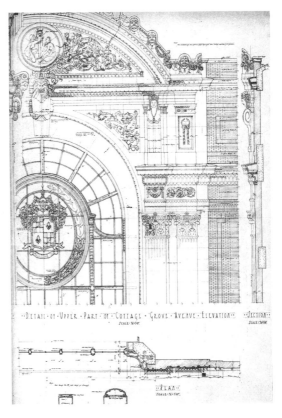

The Tivoli facade drawn in the Beaux Arts way
showing plan, elevation and section. The plan is
a view from above while the section matches the
facade details from the side. Rapp & Rapp didn't
need to draw all the detail to make it plain enough
for on-site workmen. (Rapp Collection)

grand lobby evoked the 17th century Chapel of Versailles with a staircase at one end in place of the
sacred altar. While the earlier Champaign Orpheum was a smaller adaptation of Versailles' La Salle
de Spectacle, the Tivoli's grand lobby was larger than the original chapel and, as a technically modern
adaptation to modern needs rather than a direct copy, a good deal different in treatment.

B & K and the Rapps didn't make many fundamental mistakes, but they got too far ahead of public
tastes when the Chicago and Tivoli initially favored movies over stage shows. The two theatres were
built with orchestra pits recessed into the stage, which compressed the space for live shows. This left
only a small center stage with reduced areas near the wings. The idea had been to bring audiences
closer to the small movie screens of the day. Corrections soon were made at the cost of some seating. The stage was extended, the seats moved back, and live shows went on.[1] Popular organ concerts
and the biggest names in entertainment continued to share the limelight with feature films. B&K as
well as other owner/operators continually revised and updated their theatres as needed; whether for
more seating, a better marquee, bigger concession stands, fire code revisions or timely adjustments
to public tastes.

The Tivoli's Grand Lobby, very much in the spirit of the Versailles Chapel but larger. (Rapp Collection).

Grand Dome of the Tivoli Theatre. (Rapp Collection)

The Tivoli stage and proscenium arch flanked by the decorative organ-pipe screens, all swathed in drapery. The recessed stage proved too small for elaborate stage productions and was quickly enlarged. (Rapp Collection)

This may be the most stately space Rapp & Rapp ever created; the Tivoli's Music Room bathed in light from the arched front window above the exterior marquee. (Rapp Collection)

C. W. Rapp and Barney Balaban seemed an unlikely pair; Rapp a plain spoken commercial architect from southern Illinois and the 27-years-younger Balaban a thoroughly religious Jew from a Chicago immigrant neighborhood. It turned out that the two were pretty much of a piece; both straightforward and even blunt businessmen who shared basic assumptions and kept their agreements. Barney Balaban was B&K's genius who spent many days with C. W. huddled over a drafting table in Rapp's bare office in the top floor of the State-Lake Building. Often they took long lunches together at Balaban's Standard Club, a Jewish club at 24th Street and Michigan Avenue. Together they faced the endless problems of creating new temples of entertainment, and since Balaban was in debt anyway, cost ceased to be an object. The imaginative Balaban sometimes got ahead of himself, and Rapp would say something like: If you're the architect you don't need me. At such moments Balaban backed away, but frequently he sought another authority by pulling aside any workman on the job to ask if he liked a certain treatment. If not, Balaban was known to order the offending portion torn out. To him the common man was the potential customer who knew best. "Movies are for the masses," said B&K's president David Wallerstein in the 1960s,[2] echoing what had become industry-wide commonplace. Abe Balaban's idea of every man as king was policy at B&K, which meant tickets were never sold on a reserved basis. One price got you any seat in the house; first come, first served.

The Mausoleum in the Jewish Waldheim Cemetery designed for Barney Balaban in 1923 by
C. W. & Geo. L. Rapp. (Chicago History Museum)

Rapp and Barney Balaban's mutual respect was fundamental to the success of the architecture, and Balaban even hired Rapp to design his family mausoleum, a pharaonic crypt in the Jewish Waldheim Cemetery in Forest Park south of Chicago. Rapp & Rapp designed nearly all of B&K's major theatres with the notable exception of John Eberson's immense atmospheric Paradise (1928) on Chicago's west side; and this perhaps only because C.W. Rapp had died just before the Paradise work began. "Atmospheric" describes a style that sought an outdoor illusion of palatial walled gardens, with clouds and twinkling stars overhead. The style was used by Rapp & Rapp only sparingly but was Chicago architect Eberson's trademark. Eberson was one of the "big four" palace architects of the period, which included the Rapps, Thomas Lamb and C. Howard Crane who designed more theatres than any of the others.

Before a job the principals of Balaban & Katz and Rapp & Rapp typically met around a conference table in B&K's office, ultimately located upstairs in the Chicago Theatre. Barney Balaban, the man

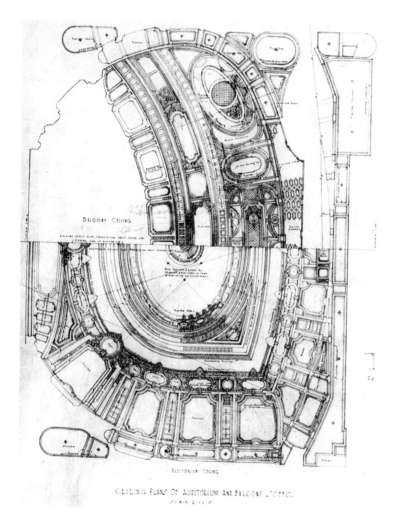

Chicago Theatre with the original marquee. (Rapp Collection)

Chicago Theatre ceiling and soffit plans. Designers routinely drew only a partial depiction of ornament. Full development through an area was needlessly time-consuming. (Rapp Collection)

who signed the checks, presided. After all the negotiating and presenting Balaban finally would ask, "Has everyone finished his chiseling?" If no one spoke he declared the meeting adjourned. Without lawyers and contracts C. W. Rapp and Balaban would shake hands and the deal was done.

The Chicago Theatre was always C. W. Rapp's favorite job, probably because of its many innovations. First among these was a visually spectacular wide-span balcony built without vertical supports, allowing unobstructed sight lines from any seat in the house. The technology supporting this cantilevered balcony allowed the theatre to be wider than deep, bringing the audience closer to the stage. The free-span balcony was particularly breathtaking to the 1921 public who had never seen such a thing. View-obstructing balcony support columns had always been a necessary fault of theatres. Compared to the old way of pillars and posts, the Chicago's balcony seemed to counter the law of gravity. No one in authority was ready to accept that such a huge apparently unsupported long span would hold the weight of 1,500 patrons. C.W. Rapp's assurances were not enough to convince, and before city inspectors approved any job they required routine load-deflection tests.

These were achieved by first nailing abutting boards marked in matching increments to the sidewalls and balcony. Sand bags were loaded on by the hundreds while officials checked for any separation of the board markings. City officials around the country routinely demanded similar deflection tests wherever there was an apparently unsupported span. As C. W. always predicted there was only minimal deflection. What appeared an act of massive levitation was not magic. The secret lay with three truss cantilevers tied-in to a steel and concrete cross beam, giving the balcony more support than

The Chicago's huge steel-supported balcony span amazed the public and inspired disbelief among city officials in 1921. The cantilever technology allowed the architects to bring audiences closer to the stage by designing the house wider than it was deep, giving an intimate feel to a large space. (Rapp Collection)

Load-deflection tests were required by city governments to prove that theatre balconies could support the weight of audiences. This one in the smaller Aurora Paramount was comparatively modest. (Chicago History Museum)

it would ever need. A common piece of engineering today, cantilever construction on such a scale was new and breathtaking in 1919 when the Chicago was built.

The three big balcony trusses were fabricated to office specifications in an East St. Louis foundry and trucked to Chicago overnight on tandem flat bed trailers. George Rapp sent a man down to oversee and sign-off on the transfer, and to ride home with the cargo. On the return trip one of the covering tarpaulins broke free causing the caravan to pull over while the crew re-secured the canvas. George's man took it on himself to ride the rest of the way outside in the damp night to tend the lines on route, an initiative that got him pneumonia from which he died within days. George was upset by the outcome, and even more disturbed when told that some around the office blamed him for the man's death. Apologetically he replied, "I never told him to ride on top." Despite this off-site mishap the overall safety record at Rapp & Rapp was good, but blemished in 1930 when a plaster worker stepped off a catwalk and fell to his death through the Southtown Theatre ceiling.

By virtue of their size, the Tivoli and Chicago created greater crowd circulation problems than had the Central Park. Rapp & Rapp solved the logistical problems of continuous day and evening performances by creating large lobbies, cross-aisles, exit passageways called vomitories and side stairways, all designed to keep arriving and departing patrons out of one another's way. Always at the front of every official mind was the memory of Chicago's 1903 Iroquois Theatre fire that claimed lives for lack of good exits. Modern theatres met the new fire codes by using ten ton stage-front concrete or steel fire curtains requiring heavy compressors to raise and lower, and a plethora of marked doors whose decorative "Exit" signs gave rise to a minor design art form.

Air-conditioning too was a movie house breakthrough and a prime marketing tool for management who advertised the theatres as oases during long hot summers in a time when home and workplace cooling was only a wish. The Chicago Theatre's clever system pulled 50 degree air from the city's honeycomb of subterranean freight tunnels, passed the air through scrubbers and forced it into the house through under-seat registers called mushrooms.

From the time of ancient Egypt, architects have been called the master builders. They are the ultimate supervisors responsible for a job's every aspect, always open to first blame and last criticism while most of the credit passes to the project owners. Rapp & Rapp and most other architects of the time understood the idea of putting forward the man who paid them. If the Rapps signed their work at all it was in the form of a modest plaque affixed to the backstage lighting panel inscribed "C. W. & Geo. L. Rapp, Architects." With the Chicago, Tivoli and the many palaces that followed, the weight of responsibility was heavy, each one a process of brutally detailed work. Often managing a number of projects at the same time, the architects started every job with proposals and working drawings subject to change-orders even before construction began.

Initial bidding from contractors could delay a job from the start, since they never came back all at once. On a big job, bidding procedures could go on for a month or more. From the beginning everyone seemed to have an opinion, from the owners and operators to workmen, projectionists and ushers. Specifications addenda and change-orders began to pile up early, and the first of many corrective "pasters" to follow were affixed to various areas of the linen drawings from which blueprints were made. To avoid more troubles later, the architects stretched these preparatory tasks as long as possible before signing the general contract. The Balabans, but not all clients, were willing to allow time to get things right early on.

Before construction began, Rapp & Rapp had hooded and fenced the sidewalks, closed-off alleys, shored up nearby structures and arranged for buildings next door to reinforce common walls. They razed existing buildings, cleared and graded the site, took test borings to determine

Chicago's Grand Staircase with its turned railing rising three levels. (Rapp Collection)

substrata, constructed building elevators and brought in cranes. Then at last they opened the hole, starting construction from the caissons, piers and sub-grid foundations. Next they poured the foundation and began the steel framing. The office had to arrange with the city for times to receive materials into the job, scheduling when they could bring concrete trucks to the site and establishing hours to get things in and done without permits. It never hurt that the Balabans knew people at city hall when a job might have needed six yards of concrete at mid-day, sometimes with a motorcycle escort.

Meanwhile many special finishing materials needed throughout the big theatres had to be selected, a process that started almost immediately and continued to the last wall sconce. The tasks included reviewing dozens of special marble samples, vast swathes of drapery material, upholsteries and floor and stair carpeting, some of which was specially loomed. The looms for carpeting may have run only infrequently which meant estimating how much extra product might be necessary to store away for future repairs of high traffic areas. Movie palace drapery became more elaborate than anything gone before. House drapery—called drapes in the industry—gave life and warmth to interior architecture while spectacular stage drapes, called "tormentors" and "teasers," parted like heaven's gates from

center stage to the wings, or rose to the proscenium arch in layers of dramatic swags. The
varied fabrics of these specially designed drapes
had to be selected with care and lots of planning. Marble may have been Travertine, Carrara
or the faux material called scagliola made of
plaster, resins and marble dust to finish like the
real thing. Much hardware was stock from suppliers but much else had to be imported, with
still more custom-made. All this took time and
required special insights into providing clients
with what they needed even before they knew
it.

Interior ornament, especially ornamental plaster,
gave unique life and presence to every theatre,
and its application needed close supervision by
managers from the office who went out to work
with molders on the job. As the job progressed,
photographs depicting ornamental segments
were provided daily to the office and reviewed
by the designers and principals. Arthur Adams'
designers couldn't turn out enough drawings to
make every detail apparent, nor was it necessary
beyond indicating motifs and marking for repetition through a course of ornament. For cast

The Grand Dome of the Chicago Theatre.
(Rapp Collection)

plaster, changes from one motif to another could be indicated in the shop drawings, and contractors
also made shop drawings from full-sized molds; though in the real world these processes weren't
always exact. If things failed to come out even, plasterers on site used wet material to squeeze or ease
a foot here and there to avoid expensive re-casting. Where they could the Rapps used catalog plaster
castings produced in local shops. For site-specific work they needed skilled artisans, many of whom
were European immigrants raised and trained in the centuries-old techniques of relief, modeling and
sculpture, and able to shape it quickly on the job.

Major plaster pieces for the grand dome, proscenium arch, sidewalls and balcony soffits, some
weighing as much as a ton, were affixed to metal frames resembling outsized chicken wire, leaving
ribbons of heavy wire molded into the back with excelsior-like loose ends. Slowly and deliberately
the pieces were hoisted into place and tied from behind using loops of the wire ribbons, while lathers
quickly slushed the whole thing down with wet plaster. Pieces of the ceiling and grand dome were
fixed in place and suspended from the overhead structure with a forest of iron hangers called pencil
rods. Lathers wound them around with tin-coated wire and lashed them in. A clever method used to
protect gold-leaf ornament was to apply a transparent finishing solution of starch and water. When
the dirt of years began to show, the starch could be washed away and reapplied without damaging
the gold leaf.

To handle these and many other details for large out-of-town jobs Rapp & Rapp opened sub-offices usually staffed by a Chicago office representative or a local clerk-of-the-works with two or three men. This was very different from smaller projects that could develop on the job with a good set of sketches and a skeleton set of specifications. Typically it took just a year to build a theatre from drafting table to finished product. Deadlines often were pushed so hard that the opening night audience was arriving at the box office as the last of the painters left by the back door. For most projects a full set of drawings done with ink on linen for durability included architecturals (floor plans, front elevations and side-view sections), mechanicals (heating, air conditioning, plumbing) and electricals (circuitry and lighting), owner's copies of which were presented at the end of every job. For the Chicago and Tivoli's mechanical and electrical drawings Rapp & Rapp contracted the structural engineering firm Lieberman, Klein & Hein, with offices in the State-Lake Building just below the Rapps. The firm later became Lieberman & Hein, used by Rapp & Rapp for many of the big jobs of the 1920s.

Rapp & Rapp's typical fee was six percent—sometimes more, sometimes less—of a job's total cost. Sometimes the office accepted paper in lieu of cash, either project bonds or promissory notes, for a percentage of future profits. In all they were well paid for their many troubles. There were few better business risks than movie houses during the Roaring Twenties.

5 | THE COLORADO RAPPS

The Panama-California Exposition, commonly called the San Diego Fair, opened in 1915 to celebrate completion of the Panama Canal, a flexing of American muscle following the Spanish-American War that set the nation's purposeful tone for the following half century. The baroque Spanish Colonial architecture and gardens dominating the 640-acre fairgrounds was a change from the Greco-Roman classicism at the Chicago World's Fair of 1893 and the St. Louis Fair of 1904. The San Diego concept was the inspiration of chief architect Bertram Grosvenor Goodhue of New York who, like the early Rapp architects except for George, had no school of architecture degree. Remembered as a modernist by virtue of his design for the towering Nebraska State Capitol (1920), Goodhue nevertheless had the soul of a lyric poet when in 1915 he wrote of the San Diego Fair site in terms that may seem remote today:

"Judged by all ordinary and extraordinary canons of beauty, the regions that may, because of their climate, foliage, color and form, be held to be loveliest are but few in number—the Riviera, the Bay of Naples and Salerno, some of the Greek Islands, certain mountain valleys in India, the Vega of Granada, the parallel one of Shiraz. In Southern California may be found every attraction possessed by those cited—the tenderest of skies, the bluest of seas, mountains of perfect outline, the richest of sub-tropical foliage... In the midst of this beauty lies the city of San Diego, the nearest Pacific port in the United States to the western end of the Panama Canal."[1]

In keeping with this vision the dome and tower of the exposition's California State Building and Quadrangle as seen from the approach across the Puente Cabrillo were glistening apparitions recalling Moorish Spain and the colonial citadels of Mexico. Below were the Prado Arcade on La Laguna de las Flores, the botanical gardens, the Plaza de Panama, and the Foreign Arts Building reminiscent

The State of California Building at San Diego's Panama-California Exposition of 1915. Designed by the fair's chief architect Bertram Grosvenor Goodhue, this building typified the dominant architectural scheme of the fair. (Elder Publishers)

of the Hospital de Santa Cruz at Toledo. There was the Canadian Building, the Prado Esplanade and the arcade flowing with drapery of the Foreign and Domestic Building. Out of place in evoking a simpler heritage was the State of New Mexico Building designed by C. W. and George Rapp's brothers under the separate firm of I H. & W. M. Rapp and A. C. Hendrickson, Architects and Superintendents Specializing in Public Buildings, Trinidad, Colorado. Rustic beside its churrigueresque neighbors the New Mexico Building was a recollection of the kind at Isleta and the old Franciscan and Indian mission of San Esteban del Rey at Acoma pueblo. According to archaeologist Sylvanus Griswold Morley, who knew the Rapps, the Acoma Indians began building San Esteban del Rey in 1629, directed by Fray Juan Ramirez.

The Rapps' New Mexico pavilion featured rough and irregular adobe-like exterior walls (brick finished with stucco) pierced by viga ends (extensions of the interior beams) that cast slow-shifting shadows with the turning of the earth. The front elevation featured short and stout twin towers joined by a second floor loggia, and inside were the favored Rapp woodwork and fireplaces. The purity and human scale of the Pueblo Revival style captured the imagination of fair-goers and critics alike.

This modest pavilion at the edge of the Balboa Park fair site was the second incarnation of a design the Rapps did in 1908 for C.M. Schenk's Colorado Supply Company building in Morley, Colorado. In 1916 it appeared for a third time in downtown Santa Fe as the city's art museum, which underwent a tasteful restoration/renovation in the 1980s spearheaded by Nat Owings, retired of Skidmore, Owings & Merrill. Planned as a city focal point for exhibits and concerts, architect Antoine Predock carried out the renovation with a building addition by Edward Larrabee Barnes Associates.[2]

The unassuming original of 1915 in San Diego, begun in a Colorado coal mining camp, captured the sense of the American Southwest more durably than Bertram Goodhue's grander California Colonial Revival. An earlier I. H & W. M. Rapp Spanish Mission style New Mexico Building designed for the 1904 Louisiana Purchase Centennial Exposition in St. Louis might have been more in keeping with Goodhue's California Colonial plan, but far less distinctive than the desert-haunted nativism that emerged quietly at the San Diego Fair in the same year C. W. and George Rapp accomplished a defining style of their own with the Al. Ringling Theatre in Baraboo, Wisconsin.

A view of the New Mexico Building under construction at the San Diego Fair, photographed by archaeologist Jesse Nussbaum in 1915. Nussbaum knew the Rapps and acted as job site superintendent. This Rapp and Hendrickson Pueblo Revival style structure recalled a heritage different from the dominant California Colonial buildings favored by the fair's lead architect Bertram Goodhue. (Courtesy Palace of the Governors Photo Archive [NMHM/DCA]. Negative # 060255)

The Baptist Church (1885), Anthony, Kansas, I. H. Rapp's first job with partner Clarence Bulger. (Fletcher Collection)

One of Bulger & Rapp's early jobs in Trinidad, Zion's Lutheran Church, 1889. (Fletcher Collection)

Trinidad's Holy Trinity Catholic Church rectory, a 1913 job by I. H. & W. M. Rapp and A. C. Hendrickson. (Fletcher Collection)

Some people today look back with moral regret on America's westward expansion, apparently ignoring where they might be if it had never happened; but years before the San Diego Fair eldest Rapp brother Isaac Hamilton viewed the winning of the West as opportunity. Hometown Carbondale couldn't provide enough work for both his father and him so Ham followed the rails west, first to Anthony, Kansas, in 1885, the year the federal government declared the western frontier officially settled. By summer of 1891 he formed Trinidad, Colorado's Rapp & Rapp firm with his brother William Mason Rapp (1863–1920), the partnership most remembered for their evocative Santa Fe style, as the Pueblo Revival architecture came to be known, named after the city that most reflects and protects its influence. In fact I. H. & W. M Rapp did much more over the years by designing in a variety of styles at least 150 commercial, municipal and religious buildings that brought urban structure to the growing areas of Colorado and New Mexico. The western Rapps were so restless and productive that the complete extent of their work still is unknown.

They built theatres as well, at the same time the Chicago Rapps were just beginning: the West (Fox) Theatre, Trinidad (1907–08); the Elks Theatre, Santa Fe (1911); the Shuler in Raton, New Mexico (1914–15) and the Star Theatre, Walsenburg, Colorado (1917). Hamilton Rapp with his first partner Clarence Bulger preceded these with the Opera House (1887) in Anthony, Kansas. The Rapp brothers' father Isaac (1830–1913) got into theatre work himself in 1894 when he designed and built a 500-seat vaudeville house above Carbondale's First National Bank, described in the newspapers as "elegant" and fitted with "the finest lighting system in southern Illinois."

Trinidad's West Theatre was not named for its location but after its founder Ed West who

West-Fox Theatre, Trinidad, built by I. H. & W. M. Rapp in 1907-08. (Fletcher Collection)

Opera House in Anthony, Kansas, built by Bulger & Rapp in 1887. According to a news account of the day Mrs. I. H. Rapp played the piano on opening night. (Fletcher Collection)

The Shuler Theatre, Raton, originally was part of a civic center plan including city hall and firehouse that later vacated the building. Today the restored Shuler is home to a performing arts company (Fletcher Collection)

Shuler Theatre interior, Raton, New Mexico, built in 1914-15 by I. H. & W. M. Rapp. (Raton Arts Council)

hired the Rapps and their draftsman A. C. Hendrickson. The theatre seated 600 on the orchestra floor, 250 in the balcony and 350 in the second balcony gallery. The basement contained a 50 by 75 foot ballroom, a ladies retiring room, a gentlemen's smoking room and a kitchen. The theatre's entrance hallway was flanked by storefronts. Like the giant theatres to come from their brothers C. W. & Geo. L. Rapp, the West hosted a range of touring stage shows, which ultimately gave way to motion pictures. Today the West-Fox continues to show movies as Colorado's oldest and largest theatre in continuous operation from opening day.

In 1888 when Bulger & Rapp had left Kansas for Colorado they had no idea what the future would bring, but they recognized good potential in Trinidad's situation as division point for the Santa Fe Railroad. Located in the high desert foothills of the Rockies near Raton Pass at the northern New Mexico border, Trinidad lay along the Purgatory River (called the Purgatoire or "Picketwire") within the Vigil and St. Vrain Land Grant. The town billed itself "Gateway to the Rocky Mountains" and as a rich source of silica, fire clay and native sandstone. Trinidad coal and coke were used to stoke furnaces in buildings and mills across the country, local plants used home-made coke to manufacture paving bricks for new roads east and west (I.H. remembered seeing Trinidad bricks in Carbondale's streets) and the rails supported a modern and growing cattle industry. Ham saw a vibrant town with a broad future and a proud past, later symbolized by its public bronze of pioneer Indian fighter Kit Carson, and registered in local memory by the presence not many years before of dime novel legends Wyatt Earp and Bat Masterson. To Rapp, Trinidad seemed ideally cradled between two landmark Rocky Mountain foothills called Fisher's Peak and Simpson's Rest, burial place of early pioneer George S. Simpson. In the distance brooded the saw-toothed range of the Sangre de Christo Mountains and the great twin Spanish Peaks.

When they got to Trinidad in 1888, Bulger & Rapp took a space in the Bell Block office of realtor C. T. Quisenberry and bought a one column by one-inch ad in the Daily Citizen newspaper. Promoting themselves as architects and superintendents specializing in modern residences, they quickly got much more than they expected. Between 1888 when they built the local firehouse and 1890, the new architects in town provided Trinidad with more than thirty buildings, a surprising output in just two years. They applied various architectural styles to barns, homes, schools, churches, a jail, industrial coke ovens and even southern Colorado's first reform synagogue. In 1899 they left their cramped quarters in Quisenberry's office and took a room in the Bloom Block. Successful though it was, the Bulger & Rapp partnership was short lived. Clarence Bulger could never shake his altitude sickness, called mountain fever, which finally forced him to leave Trinidad for Texas where with his son he continued to practice architecture. I. H. Rapp worked with Bulger again on some Texas projects but never again as an official partner.

Will Rapp's first look at Trinidad occurred when father Isaac and he paid a visit to I. H. Rapp In August, 1890, likely to get the old man's opinion of the city as a place to do business. Isaac Rapp's operating rule of life was to live where the work is. Evidently he approved, and the new partnership of I. H. & W. M. Rapp began in 1891 by finishing what Bulger & Rapp had begun, the Richardsonian Romanesque First National Bank Building at the central downtown corner of Main and Commercial. The Bulger & Rapp bank originally was planned as a four story building but by August of that year they added a fifth floor to the design. Though the site was excavated in October

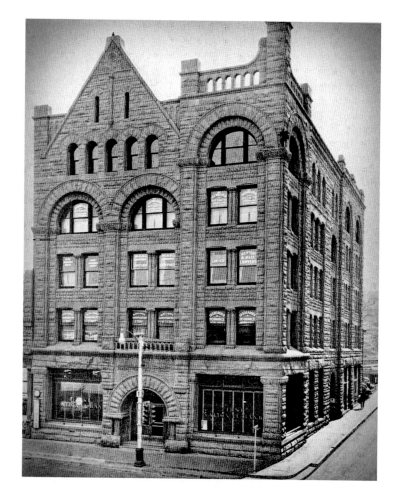

First National Bank in Trinidad (1892), I. H. & W. M. Rapp's first job together as partners. (Rapp Collection)

1890, construction didn't start until March 1891, the month Bulger left Trinidad for Galveston. Will Rapp joined his brother to complete the $120,000 building for the bank's opening in May 1892.

In the same year the Rapp brothers expanded their Bloom Block quarters to two rooms. In April 1905 they moved into new offices in suite 3 on the second floor of the McCormick Building, named for its owner David W. McCormick, located across the intersection from the First National Bank. The Rapps bought the McCormick with four adjoining buildings in October 1901 for $38,000 and reworked the facades to make all the buildings appear as one. The Main Street side was stripped and rebuilt in 1902. In 1906 the office remodeled the Commercial Street elevation, completed in January 1907. In the midst of this work, in February 1906, W. M. Rapp bought the nearby Turner-Ford Building for $35,000. The McCormick, Turner-Ford and others in Trinidad were Will Rapp's pet projects. He spent many careful hours working-out the plans and even went back to Chicago to consult with his brother Cornelius Ward. Will always had the idea of making his architecture work for him, and developing commercial income-producing properties was always high in his mind.

In 1912 the Rapp office moved once again, this time into the local Masonic Building they designed in 1910 and finished in 1911. On the night of May 11 of that year a fire ravaged the office, destroying a wealth of architectural plans and records. Rapp & Rapp quickly rebuilt and remained in the

The Masonic Building in Las Vegas, New Mexico, built by I. H. & W. M. Rapp and dedicated June 24, 1895. (Fletcher Collection)

Masonic Building to 1925 when the firm moved across the street into the Turner-Ford Building. Charles Rapp, the banker brother of the architects, continued in the Turner office as property manager for the Rapp interests until his death in 1951.

In addition to these Trinidad locations I. H. & W. M. Rapp kept local offices near centers of work in Las Vegas and Santa Fe, New Mexico. I. H. Rapp maintained the one in Santa Fe, which suffered another serious fire in 1914, costing the office a trove of watercolors and architectural plans worth "hundreds of dollars," according to the Santa Fe New Mexican. The Rapps' Santa Fe offices, run by Ham, operated from 1897 to 1899 and again from 1909 to 1924. William Mason lived and ran a busy Rapp & Rapp office in Las Vegas, New Mexico from 1895 to 1897 and again from 1899 to 1907. The Rapps' first major structure in the "Meadow City" was the three-story Masonic Building, designed in 1892 and after delays completed June 24, 1895. The Las Vegas Optic newspaper praised the building by writing "I. H. Rapp has personally and faithfully supervised every part of the construction, with the result that the Temple is one of the best built structures in New Mexico."

During the early Bulger & Rapp years in Anthony, Will Rapp worked at Chicago's Holabird and Roche, as had his brother Cornelius Ward before him. After a doctor suggested that a drier climate might help Will's skin and bronchial problems, he left Chicago to join an architect in Wichita, spending holidays in nearby Anthony with Ham and his wife Jean Morrison Rapp. Ham had married Jean in 1886 at her Odin, Illinois, family home where she was known in that small town near Centralia as Miss Jennie.

Isaac Hamilton Rapp was named after his father Isaac and grandfather Alexander Hamilton Rapp, born in 1808 and named for New York's representative to the Constitutional Convention and first U. S. treasury secretary. Will Rapp was named after Massachusetts locomotive designer William Mason (1808–1883), creator of engines for the Illinois Central Railroad which passed through Carbondale. Isaac Rapp respected Mason's creations, which had an industrial-strength impressiveness expressing the designer's idea that locomotives "should look somewhat better than cook stoves on wheels."[3] One of his iron beauties pulled Abraham Lincoln's funeral train back to Springfield where in earlier days Lincoln had been an attorney for the Illinois Central.

Detail of an of A. C. Hendrickson rendering used by Will Rapp to sell the commercial concept of Pueblo Revival to officials in Santa Fe, New Mexico. (Rapp Collection)

Mr. and Mrs. Arthur C. Hendrickson. He was hired as I. H. & W. M. Rapp's chief draftsman in 1900 and became full partner in 1909. (Colorado Historical Society)

Will Rapp tended more to civic boosterism than any of his brothers. In this he followed his father Isaac who early in his career collected donations in Carbondale for a fund which paid him to rebuild a burned college structure. That same kind of constructive salesmanship showed in Will after Santa Fe's city fathers saw the Rapps' Morley, Colorado, building and found it "in the spirit" of what was needed for a distinctive municipal development plan. Will Rapp paid a visit to the enthusiastic officials in Santa Fe, carrying proposals and four watercolor renderings done in the Pueblo Revival style by A. C. Hendrickson.

Arthur C. Hendrickson from Beloit, Wisconsin, settled in Las Vegas, New Mexico, where I. H. and W. M. Rapp maintained a busy office. He joined the Rapps in 1900 and became chief draftsman in the Trinidad office, which he held together while Hamilton Rapp worked in Santa Fe and Will Rapp in Las Vegas. Hendrickson conceived the Pueblo Revival style for the Morley mining camp in 1908, taking off from the Mission style New Mexico Building the office had done for the 1904 St. Louis fair. Hendrickson became a full partner in 1909, which changed the official name of the firm to I. H. & W. M. Rapp and A. C. Hendrickson, Architects.

La Fonda Hotel, Santa Fe, New Mexico, as it appeared before the Meem-Colter additions. I. H. & W. M. Rapp and A. C. Hendrickson began design and construction work in the spring of 1920 and completed the job in February, 1922. The hotel opened in December of that year. (Fletcher Collection)

The country club building at Trinidad Municipal Golf Course was the last Pueblo Revival structure done by the Rapp office. It was completed in 1922 shortly following the deaths in quick succession of Will Rapp and Arthur Hendrickson, the firm's biggest boosters of the Santa Fe style. (Fletcher Collection)

This view captures the mood and vision of the Pueblo Revival style as realized in the Trinidad Country Club, photographed by Will Rapp's grandson William Mason Rapp in 2004. (Rapp Collection)

Hendrickson's renderings, heavily promoted in Santa Fe by Will Rapp, successfully demonstrated how low profile Pueblo Revival buildings might be developed for commercial and professional offices. The Rapp firm applied this style a number of times in Santa Fe including La Fonda Hotel, finished in 1922 after the deaths of W. M. Rapp and A. C. Hendrickson. La Fonda resulted after years of official debate in Santa Fe over the need for a new hotel to attract tourism. After a 1919 subscription drive to finance the job, the board of directors in February 1920 interviewed prospective hotel managers and even other architects. The Rapps and Hendrickson used a terraced Pueblo Revival scheme. Younger designers John Gaw Meem and Mary Colter made a large addition to the hotel in 1929. I. H. Rapp might have been called in for the addition but by then he had long since abandoned the style. The last Pueblo Revival design produced by the Rapp office was the country club building at Trinidad's Municipal Golf Course. Work on the club building, designed by Hendrickson, began in November 1920 after La Fonda Hotel construction was under way and was finished April 4, 1921, a few months before Hendrickson's death. In effect, for Rapp & Rapp, the Santa Fe style began and ended in Colorado, appearing first in Morley and last in Trinidad. Ham dropped the scheme forever after 1923 write-ups on the country club's distinctive Pueblo Revival design appearing in Denver's Rocky Mountain News, Architectural Record, Golf Digest and American Golfer magazine encouraged other architects to pursue the style.

Most notable among these newcomers was John Gaw Meem, who encountered the style as a young tuberculosis patient at Santa Fe's Sunmount Sanatorium, a pure Pueblo Revival structure built by Rapp & Rapp in 1914. Meem said the building's tranquility made him want to become an architect.[4] He and others, including designer Mary Elizabeth Jane Colter, took the Santa Fe style, squared off the corners and carried it on into the 1950s. The results increasingly became more self-conscious and the style more modern, at the cost of its early wind-eroded presence.

Will Rapp was a compulsive tinkerer frequently at the forefront of Trinidad civic projects. He was a Mason, an Elk, an Episcopalian, a charter member of Trinidad's Rotary Club, a city council member, director of the Trinidad National Bank, and for amusement (like his father who never gave it up) a dedicated weekend wood-

C. H. Nichols and W. M. Rapp were partners in local real estate including this Nichols-Rapp garage. This building was the last Rapp-owned property in Trinidad when it was sold in the 1980s; a century after I. H. Rapp arrived in the southern Colorado city. (Rapp Collection)

worker. He also enthusiastically promoted Trinidad's McCormick block. Will went back to Chicago to consult with his brother Cornelius Ward on the McCormick plan and to press for his brother's investment in the commercial project. In following letters Will repeatedly and without result urged C.W. to come west to show more interest in his investment. Among still other things, Will had a half interest with local businessman C. H. Nichols in a vehicle storage business that came to called Nichols-Rapp Garage, noteworthy only because of its longevity. Absentee half interest in Nichols-Rapp came down profitless through the family to the 1980s, long after the Rapps had gone from Trinidad and the principals from this world.

Will Rapp had faith that hard work, friendship and civic involvement could make a city grow and improve every life. He went directly for the "new," always thinking and planning ahead. He bought the best and liked to be first. According to his son Mason, Will had the first automobile in town (a 1910 Franklin), the first Victrola (he liked Tchaikovsky's Waltz of the Flowers on Christmas morning especially) and was among the first to get an outlying weekend home in nearby Stonewall, an area near Monument Lake. At the doorstep of the Sangre de Christo Mountains, Stonewall's higher elevation provided Trinidad's wealthier residents a pleasant summer escape from the city heat. In his Stonewall house Will created the first ice-free refrigerator in the area by diverting a cold underground stream through a locker he installed beneath the kitchen floor. Will wrote to his young son Mason in 1920, "We are going to build a hangar for all airplanes out beyond the hospital, so Trinidad is to have a flying field. If this goes through I suppose we will be taking trips up to Stonewall in a flying machine."

Always eager for the future, Will invested in railroad and Arizona copper-mining stock and bought tracts of coal property between

The impressive home the Rapps built for prominent Trinidad businessman C. H. Nichols, now a bed and breakfast called Stone Mansion. (Ken Fletcher Photo)

Colorado Fuel & Iron holdings near neighboring Walsenburg, believing that some day the huge producer owned by the Rockefellers would have to buy him out at higher prices. He partnered on buying speculative Trinidad property with local businessman C. H. Nichols, for whom the Rapps built one of the city's most impressive homes. Planning for wider development, he also bought land around Las Vegas, New Mexico. Will Rapp seemed willing to own anything but his family home in Trinidad at Chestnut and 3rd, which inexplicably he continued to rent. Perhaps he always planned to build his own.

I. H. and Jean Rapp had lived in Santa Fe and returned from there to Trinidad in 1924, where they bought the home known as the Hammerslough house at 2nd and Chestnut, only a block from Will's family home. Ham's house wasn't a Rapp design but he did add a breakfast room in the rear. Will Rapp lived in Las Vegas, New Mexico, from 1899 until March 1903, when he moved to Trinidad and became a member of the chamber of commerce. In August of that year he took a trip to Stonewall with a group that included his future bride Mary, daughter of prominent Trinidad businessman Pasquale Gerardi.

No matter where the Rapps lived or traveled as work demanded, their main office was always in Trinidad with A. C. Hendrickson left in charge. In those days of difficult and slow transportation over long and dusty distances the Rapp partners traveled so widely and often in the course of business in Colorado, New Mexico and Texas, that it is hard to imagine how they found the time—not to mention the problems they faced transporting materials to far-flung construction sites. Before gasoline-powered trucking, all was managed with horse teams and wagons moving out from the nearest railroad hubs through heat, cold, dust and mud.

In his unrelenting effort to plan ahead, Will Rapp didn't always get it right. Trinidad pumped sufficient water from Monument Lake thirty miles away, but Rapp believed tourism and development could be improved by promoting clear mountain water brought down from picturesque Fisher's Peak. In a miscalculation supported by enthusiasm, he designed an elaborate mountainside sluice and pipeline which at official opening ceremonies blew up under pressure, soaked the gathered city fathers and doused the spirit of the occasion—along with any hope for the project's completion.

6 | EAST & WEST

Because most architects in those days sought to put owners first and take credit last, I. H. & W. M. Rapp rarely were quoted in newspapers and never bragged, but in June 1900 the Santa Fe New Mexican did it for them. In an embarrassment of praise the paper compared I. H. and W. M. Rapp to Sir Christopher Wren, architect of St. Paul's Cathedral, London, by repeating Wren's famous statement, "If you seek my monument, look around you."

The inspiration for this high praise was the Rapps' New Mexico Territorial Capitol Building (New Mexico, still a territory from the Mexican War of 1846–48, didn't become the 47th state until 1912). The Rapps' capitol building was preceded by one built in 1886 which burned just six years later. In August 1895 the Capitol Rebuilding Board contracted with the Rapps to draft plans for a new and grand replacement. By the following spring the board accepted the plan and, as reported by the New Mexico Optic, offered I. H. Rapp "hearty congratulation from all members on the completeness and originality of the work."

The building's opening and dedication were marked by a gala parade with Ham and Will Rapp riding in a carriage with local dignitaries. The chief justice spoke in the new hall of the House of Representatives, predicting the building's walls might last as long as Rome's seven hills.[1] Neoclassical Beaux-Arts as practiced by the Rapps was apt to inspire such grand sentiments, as happened again when the Rapps built the porticoed Territorial Governor's Mansion (1908) and Trinidad's Las Animas County Courthouse (1912). While the courthouse still endures in Trinidad, the city of Santa Fe turned unmindful of their many Rapp buildings that were not in the approved Santa Fe Style. The stately Governor's Mansion ultimately was razed, while time also had its way with the Territorial Capitol when in 1950–52 the grand building was thoroughly redesigned and the original exterior obliterated.

The Maple Street side of Las Animas County Courthouse, Trinidad. Rapp, Rapp & Hendrickson in 1915, completed the job. (Fletcher Collection)

The Las Animas county jail (at left), finished by the Rapp firm in 1918, was adjoined to the main courthouse building by an enclosed walkway. (Fletcher Collection)

I. H. & W. M. Rapp designed and built in 1900 Santa Fe's New Mexico Territorial Capitol Building. The Territory of New Mexico didn't become a state until 1912. (Fletcher Collection)

Through the years the I. H. & W. M. Rapp firm designed numerous school buildings in southern Colorado and throughout New Mexico. What became their largest campus of school buildings began in 1910 with plans for a new Trinidad high school, the three-story building shown at center. The auditorium shown at right and the gymnasium on the left were added in 1922. In 1926 the firm drew-up plans for a stadium and athletic field located below the school buildings. Only a portion of the stadium was completed. (Fletcher Collection)

The Las Animas County Courthouse job was awarded to the Rapps and Hendrickson in 1911. Applying Beaux Arts style and method, the architects began construction in June the following year and finished the building in October 1915. Work on a county jail addition to the courthouse began in 1916 and was completed in April 1918.

I. H. & W. M. Rapp's Pueblo Revival style may have established an ancient model as distinctive southwestern architecture, but they first brought their native Midwest with them. The Rapps' Romanesque First National Bank and classical Beaux Arts style Territorial Capitol and Las Animas Courthouse could have passed in Chicago. Whether East or West in origin, specific architectural styles were less important to the Rapps than the structural integrity of useful buildings, an attitude learned from their father Isaac back in Carbondale. The Chicago Rapps as well, especially C. W. who was closer to the source than younger brother George, absorbed from Isaac the same on-the-job principles about substance and permanence. C. W. internailzed the idea of permanence—he wrote of using so much steel in the Balaban & Katz theatres "that hundreds of years must pass before time will notice it."

All along, thoughts and ideas were exchanged between the Chicago and Trinidad firms via occasional train trips east and west and frequent letters. Will Rapp drew-up his McCormick Building plans on vellum during one of his visits to Chicago, while I. H. & W. M. Rapp's buildings for New Mexico Military Institute were done in a Collegiate Gothic style similar to the scheme that C. W. used in his Illinois school buildings. When the McCormick Block began to earn rental income C. W. punctually was sent his monthly share. After his death, the checks went to his widow Mary P. R. Rapp, faithfully forwarded from Trinidad by another brother, Charles Robert Rapp (1874–1951). Charles followed Ham and Will from Carbondale to Trinidad where he worked for the Trinidad National Bank. He became a bank officer and ultimately treasurer, officially titled head cashier.

Though they had offices at various times in Santa Fe and Las Vegas, New Mexico, I. H. & W. M. Rapp always claimed Trinidad as headquarters, using several locations including the third floor space in the Masonic building. Douglas McHendrie, a boyhood friend of Will's son Mason, remembered in his old age that Mase and he went to the Rice school together, got in fist fights and killed prey out at Rattlesnake Hill near Stonewall where both their parents had weekend homes. Often they ran upstairs in the Masonic Building to visit the Rapps' third floor office, which McHendrie recalled as a sprawling space with drafting tables lighted beneath low-slung green shades. Even with window exposure, the deep space of the drafting room was, according to McHendrie, "a place that always looked dark until you turned the lights on." McHendrie, whose father was a judge and who became one himself in Denver, recalled only vaguely the Rapp architects of his parents' generation, whom he said were much of the time away on business. He had a stronger recollection of the banker Charles Rapp as "the kind of man who liked to pull quarters out of your ear. Something a boy would remember."

In the course of business the Rapps got to know an influential local businessman named Pasquale (Pascal) Gerardi whose daughter W. M. Rapp would marry in 1905. Pasquale came from Viggiano, Italy; a picturesque town in the mountains above Naples. His father had settled there after coming from the north with Garibaldi's army during the Risorgimento. By way of Avignon, Marseilles, and

WEST FRONT
ON
COMMERCIAL

McCORMICK BLDG.

LOOKING
NORTHEAST

MAIN ST &
COMMERCIAL

The McCormick Building commercial block developed in 1906 and 1909 in Trinidad was the entrepreneurial Will Rapp's pet project. The McCormick was one of the income-producing properties Rapp & Rapp developed for themselves. The Rapps' Romanesque First National Bank Building is in the background of the top view, with a corner of it to the right in the second picture. These photos of the well-kept McCormick were part of an early 1950s real estate appraisal Mason Rapp had done following the death of his Uncle Charles. Bank treasurer Charles Rapp had been the local family administrator of the properties, and was the last of the Rapps to call Trinidad his home. (Rapp Collection)

Isaac Hamilton Rapp, detail from a family photo taken two years after the New Mexico Territorial Capitol and McCormick Building jobs of 1900. (Rapp Collection)

William Mason Rapp, circa 1917, in the only known picture of him in later professional life. An architect who with his brother Ham designed countless buildings for others, he was always intrigued with the promise of developments of his own. To that purpose he bought a number of properties in and around Trinidad, Colorado, and Las Vegas, New Mexico. (Rapp Collection)

Maria (Mary) Teresa Paola Gerardi, daughter of Trinidad businessman Pasquale (Pascal) Gerardi, married William (Will) Rapp in 1905. Called Grandmary by later generations of family, she was remembered by local old-timers in the 1960s as the most beautiful girl in Trinidad. (Rapp Collection)

Trinidad businessman Pasquale "Pascal" Gerardi, father of Mary Gerardi who married Will Rapp in 1905. (Gerardi-Paulin Collection)

Regina Springer Gerardi, Mary Gerardi Rapp's mother. (Gerardi-Paulin Collection)

New Oreans, Gerardi arrived in Trinidad in 1872 with only the suit he was wearing, a few dollars in his pocket and his violin. The landscape around Trinidad reminded him of home.

With traveling partner Vincent Fuccio, also from Viggiano, he borrowed funds and opened an amusement saloon on Main Street. By June the next year he ordered a $35.25 state-of-the-art billiard table from Emanuel Brunswick of Chicago. Besides pocket billiards the saloon offered wine, hard liquor and cigars along with harp and violin music provided by Fuccio and Gerardi. Pascal married a local girl named Maria Regina Springer in January 1877, two years after she was graduated from Trinidad's St. Joseph's Academy. With the respected Father C. F. Pinto officiating, the wedding was a big event that Pascal topped off by opening the doors to the "Amusement," as his saloon was known, for free liquor and cigars.

Pascal's best man was one of the last flinty American frontiersman, the aging Richens Lacey "Uncle Dick" Wootton; a man so tough he once drove 8,000 sheep from Colorado to San Francisco, taming hostile Indians along the way with fast talk and bribes of sheep. When he got to San Francisco he had 7,000 left to sell to a ready market. Wootton in 1858 opened the first saloon in Denver and was said to have owned most of the city, which he sold to move south to Trinidad. In 1866–7 he cleared trees and blasted boulders to make a passable 27-mile trail through Raton Pass south to New Mexico, whose traffic he managed by opening Raton Pass Toll Gate. Wootton's tollgate and rough road between Colorado and New Mexico operated under the Las Animas County Board of Commissioners, which Uncle Dick controlled.

Hiring a tribe of Ute Indians for labor, Wootton took significant risks to improve the way for cattle drovers through what had been the most treacherous part of the Santa Fe Trail. Passage for three span of horses or mules cost $1.00, a yoke of oxen 50 cents, each horseman 20 cents and cattle per head 2 cents. Indians, their mounts and belongings passed free. Some cattlemen objected to the fees and resisted with force of arms, but soon came to understand that it was cheaper and more comfortable to use Wootton's tollgate than find a longer way.

By the time he stood up at Pascal Gerardi's wedding, with the last of his many wives as bridesmaid, Wootton had become Trinidad's biggest booster and a popular local figure known for his ready spirit and impish sense of humor. Pascal's only son shared Wootton's middle name, though spelled differently as Vincent Lacy Gerardi. Vince became first to clear Raton Pass by automobile over Wootton's rugged road. His elder sister Mary, W. M Rapp's wife, claimed to have been the first white baby carried over Raton Pass.

Pascal left the saloon business to open a Trinidad grocery store, which expanded and improved to become Gerardi Mercantile, featuring its own convenience brand of canned and bottled foods labeled "Gerardi's Best." He served in local government and helped found the Trinidad bank. Considered a man of the people, he ran a victorious 1894 campaign for alderman against what one newspaper called the "knavish tricks" of the water works company. During a financial panic in the 1890s depositors ran to the Trinidad bank to empty their accounts, taking the proceeds to the trusted Gerardi Mercantile Company for safe-keeping. In an act of faith at incalculable personal risk Gerardi quietly saved Trinidad from itself by re-depositing the money with the bank as quickly as it came in his front door. He kept records on each deposit, and when the panic passed all the proceeds were back in the original accounts as though nothing had happened.

While W. M. Rapp had come west to find success, his wife Maria (Mary) Teresa Paola Gerardi, born in Trinidad in 1877 to Pascal and Maria Regina, seemed to identify more with the style and sophistication of the urbanized east. Along with I. H. Rapp's wife Jean, Mary cultivated a modern social circle given to luncheons, bridge tables and teas that were anything but rustic. For help with the place settings and table linen Mary hired a Mexican maid addressed as Mrs. Campas. The life was a move beyond the Santa Fe Trail heritage, Wootton's Raton Pass and the dusty piñon-dotted hills around Trinidad.

Mary's youth had been cut short when her mother died suddenly, leaving her as functional mother to Vince and their sister Kate, and she was virtually on her own at age 22 when Pascal died in 1899. She took strength less from her Catholic faith than from purposeful self-improvement. She painted still lifes, played the violin and pursued art history correspondence courses with the Art Institute of Chicago. Later on she took to the new and expensive pastime of record collecting, spending as much as $12.00 each for single-sided black lacquered 12-inch discs of Italian opera, neatly preserved in sleeved albums. Her sister-in-law Jean Rapp was a painter too, often helping Rapp draftsman A.C. Hendrickson with office renderings.

Mary and Will Rapp married in 1905 and had a son in 1906 named Mason Gerardi Rapp, called "Scrub" by his father and destined by time and heritage to become an architect. Following their marriage, Will and Mary Rapp lived in a cramped duplex on Beech Street, an investment of her father Pascal's, and stayed there until 1911 when the family moved to a permanent home at Chestnut and Third Street. Mason was followed in 1907 by sister Mary G. and a brother ten years his junior named William Hamilton, called "Billy Ham" by the family and "Billy Boy" by his father. Will called his daughter "Mary Georgeina" and always signed himself "Daddy" in letters to his children. Billy Ham's middle name was his uncle's and came from his New York great-grandfather Alexander Hamilton Rapp. He had a childhood rhyme he concocted which he liked to repeat all over the house: "Here comes the ice cream man / Combs his hair like Uncle Ham." Meaning both men were bald.

Ham and Jean Rapp had no children of their own but took in a foster daughter named Helen Hoskins after the death of her birth mother Florence (Mrs. E. T. Hoskins) in July 1903. Florence died of puerperal fever after giving birth to her seventh child. E. T. Hoskins was cashier of the San Miguel Bank, Las Vegas, New Mexico; coincidentally the same job Charles R. Rapp held at the Trinidad National Bank. Overwhelmed by his wife's death and heavy responsibility for so many children, Hoskins accepted Ham and Jean Rapp's offer to raise the second youngest child. As Helen Rapp she regularly visited her birth family in Las Vegas.

Tranquility for the Rapps and Trinidad was challenged by the infamous Colorado Coalfield War and Ludlow Massacre (1913–14) that pitted mostly immigrant coal mine workers against the Rockefellers' Colorado Fuel & Iron Company (CF&I). This might have remained a simple but sorry tale of company mismanagement had not the miners armed themselves. CF&I workers wanted better conditions and higher pay. The company adamantly refused, questioning loyalty to the company and even to

Caskets bearing the bodies of coal miners killed in the Ludlow Massacre (1914) arrive at Holy Trinity Church. I. H. & W. M. Rapp didn't build this church but they later added a steeple to it in 1904 and the rectory in 1913. (L. Dodd Photo, www.wyomingtalesandtrails.com)

Raton, New Mexico, courthouse under construction. I. H. & W. M. Rapp built it in 1897. (Fletcher Collection)

Raton Miners' Hospital (1904), another of the many jobs the Rapps did in New Mexico. (Fletcher Collection)

Home designed by I. H. & W. M. Rapp in Raton for A. L. Hobbs (1906). (Fletcher Collection)

the country of the mostly non-English-speaking middle-European immigrant work force. Sparks of violence ignited. One man was shot dead on Trinidad's Main Street and dragged away with a horse harness.

The issue became a workers' cause celebre, with the 80-year-old United Mine Workers organizer Mother Jones speaking out for the miners. Mary Harris "Mother" Jones actively took up the causes of labor after she lost her family to yellow fever and later all her belongings in the Chicago Fire of 1871. In Trinidad, Colorado she fulminated to standing-room-only crowds from the stage of I. H. & W. M. Rapp's West-Fox Theatre: "We are going to stand together and never surrender. Boys, always remember you ain't got a damn thing if you ain't got a union."[2]

In their Pueblo steel mill CF&I fabricated what the miners called the Death Special, an armored car with a machine gun turret brought to Trinidad as a menacing roving presence. State militia and finally Federal troops were called in to restore order after several miners were killed in a fiery shoot-out near the Ludlow mines just north of Trinidad. Later, Woody Guthrie wrote a sorrowful song about the incident, titled "The Ludlow Massacre."

While all this went on, the Rapps were busy putting up buildings, notably at the time the New Mexico Building for the San Diego fair. Will and Mary sheltered their two children, ages eight and six (their youngest son William Hamilton Rapp wasn't born until 1916), from all this unpleasantness, never even referring to it in their presence. The cover-up was effective, since as adults neither Mason nor Mary G. had ever heard of the Ludlow Massacre.

The Rapp-designed Carnegie Library, Raton (1911). (Fletcher Collection)

The Colorado Coalfield War was the last major disturbance in the settling areas around Trinidad, but when Isaac Hamilton Rapp arrived in 1888, ugly disputes persisted over the northern boundaries of the vast Maxwell Land Grant. At issue were a quarter million acres in southern Colorado claimed by the Land Grant and Railway Company. Central in the dispute was the Stonewall area.

Settlers throughout the region, both Anglo and Hispanic, suddenly were faced with either leaving or paying the Land Grant Company for land they had occupied for years. Three years before, the company had browbeaten settlers around Raton, New Mexico, by hiring a band of militiamen led by erstwhile Trinidad lawman Bat Masterson's brother James to enforce their edicts. North of Raton Pass in Colorado, settlers accused the company of falsifying a survey to strengthen its claim. The Company earlier had called the old pioneer Uncle Dick Wootton, among others, as a witness in the boundary dispute. Foremost among the Stonewall homestead-activists was Richard Russell and his wife Marion Sloane Russell. She grew up in the area and knew since childhood that other famous local pioneer, Kit Carson. Mary Gerardi Rapp may have been the first white baby carried over Raton Pass, but Marion Russell was among the first women to travel the entire Santa Fe Trail.

Tempers were raw over what seemed highhanded Land Grant demands when Richard Russell, followed by a crowd of armed settlers, went to meet with Land Grant and Railway officials at the Stonewall Hotel. Confusion ensued and Land Grant gunmen shot Russell to death. Marion Russell continued to press the settlers' case, but ultimately the Federal courts substantiated the Land Grant claims. Locals who stayed on had to pay for land they had developed with their own money and effort. Others who couldn't afford it, including most of the Hispanics, packed up and left.[3]

Richard Russell's killing happened in 1888, the year I. H. Rapp came to Trinidad, a town for all its promise that was still part of a Wild West not yet gone. Just nine years earlier an outfit called the

Dodge City gang had terrorized Las Vegas, New Mexico. The man who killed outlaw Jesse James by shooting him in the back and bragging about it ran a saloon in Trinidad's neighbor city Walsenburg. He left there to open a tent saloon in the nearby silver boom town of Creede, where in 1892 he himself was left for dead after a shotgun blast to the back of his head. Another part-time resident and gambler in Creede was Bat Masterson who, only six years before Hamilton Rapp arrived, was marshal of Trinidad. Another man who was by turns an outlaw and lawman was Wyatt Earp. He came to Trinidad with his brothers and the tubercular dentist turned gunman Doc Holliday after their involvement in the notorious gunfight at the OK Corral in Tombstone, Arizona, in 1881. Masterson concocted minor charges against the Earps and Holliday to prevent their extradition to Arizona on the OK Corral issue. After all this, the legendary drifters and renegade Indians around Trinidad began to disappear. Earp went to Los Angeles as consultant on movie westerns and died in 1929. Bat Masterson went to work as a newspaperman in New York City. He died in 1921.

The haphazard lawlessness personified by legendary saddle bums and gunslingers and the labor and civil strife exemplified by the Ludlow Massacre and Stonewall War were vestiges of a passing Wild West. The new West advanced by the civilizing work of I. H. & W. M. Rapp could never have happened without the troubles and trials of earlier pioneers who made final settlement possible.

7 | WAR AND THE MILITARY

Across Cornell Avenue from George Rapp's south side apartment, adjacent to the '93 World's Fair midway, lay a piece of property that was sited in 1916 for a New Windermere Hotel to be designed by C. W. & Geo. L. Rapp. The idea was to replace the old Windermere West residential hotel where George lived, with this new one at 56th Street and Jackson Park. The Rapps drew up a nine story scheme in the spirit of a palmy European spa with a wide and airy main floor lobby leading to a tea and grill room, ball room and billiard room, all graced with stately columns and ornamental enrichment. In 1917 Rapp & Rapp hired civil engineers Brussel & Vertibo for electrical and mechanical drawings, which they prepared and finished and for which they were paid; but by then the nation's entry into World War I submerged the job before it got under way. The difference between this Old World scheme and the larger modern post-war Windermere East Apartment Hotel built instead by C. W. & Geo. L. Rapp demonstrated what change a war can make. Gone were any ideas of palmy courts and leisurely walkways catering to the few. The center of social gravity shifted to America after Europe had torn itself apart. Wars and the shadows of war affected the Rapp family architects and how they built throughout the more than one hundred years they practiced, from the Civil War to the doorstep of Vietnam.

At the time of the original Windermere plan the office suspected American involvement in the Great War was coming, but life had to go on. The Windermere bowed to materials shortages just as methods had to change on the State-Lake Building and the Riviera Theatre job, Rapp & Rapp's first for Balaban & Katz. The American passenger liner Lusitania had been sunk in 1915, which alone could have justified war against Germany; but President Woodrow Wilson gave peace a chance by pushing for negotiations between the European belligerents. When Germany launched a full-fledged submarine campaign early in 1917 followed by attempts to involve Mexico against the U.S., America

Rapp & Rapp's Jackson Shore Apartments on Chicago's south side near Lake Michigan featured 24 twelve-room units. The building was completed in 1917 just before America's involvement in World War I. (Rapp Collection)

Windermere East Hotel of the post-war 1920s was by virtue of its larger scale a very different approach from the nearby Jackson Shore Apartments. The picture barely shows the Windermere West on the left, the apartment hotel where George Rapp lived. (Rapp Collection)

Windermere East veranda and vestibule. This hotel job was very different from the pre-war concept planned for the site. World War I changed the thinking. (Adams Collection)

entered the war in April. Dan Brush III went off to France as an artillery officer and McCarthy to the signal bridge of the battleship Pennsylvania. The U.S.S. Pennsylvania was one of the modern American dreadnoughts sent to aid the British Grand Fleet in the North Sea but didn't arrive until after the November 1918, Armistice. McCarthy was discharged shortly after that, though his ship went on into World War II and was severely damaged in the Japanese attack on Pearl Harbor in 1941. Following repairs the Pennsylvania served through the war in the Pacific.

Edwin C. A. (Ted) Bullock further reduced the staff at Rapp & Rapp when he left for the war as a 1st Lieutenant in the army's Tank Corps 302. He served in the Meuse Argonne and in planning a November 14, 1918 air assault on Berlin that never occurred because of the Armistice. The plan for the Berlin run was to load 500-pound bombs onto 250 aircraft, only 150 of which were expected to survive.

Other Rapp & Rapp personnel in 1917 began to filter out of the office to regular drills on the University of Chicago football field. Designer Theron Woolson was among these trainees, and in the course of the war word came to the Rapp office that he had been killed in action. The report was wrong, though at the time no one at the office knew it. After the Armistice Woolson came through the door at Rapp & Rapp looking for his old job. It was like a resurrection. C. W. hired him back and he stayed with Rapp & Rapp until 1931 when a steel strike and the Great Depression forced George to place him on "an indeterminate leave of absence" that turned out to be permanent. All Rapp employees who left for the war were given their jobs back upon return, including a valuable designer named Shaefer who lost an arm on the battlefield. His drawing arm was spared.

As to the Rapps' military background, all along there was passing talk of a family relationship to an unspecified historically renowned German general named Rapp. The only soldier with that name whose fame amounts to the colorful rumor was a German from the Alsace city of Colmar who became Napoleon's adjutant general. Count Rapp was Napoleon's favorite counsel, and on one occasion he saved the emperor's life by fighting off a battlefield assassination attempt. Accordingly there is a Paris street named for him. When Napoleon was exiled to the Island of Elba, Count Rapp went to work for the restored King Louis XVIII, which is where Rapp was found when Napoleon returned to France in 1815 for his second try at running the country. Napoleon confronted Count Rapp with a storm of questions and accusations of betrayal for having served the king in the emperor's absence. In the end Rapp replied simply, "Sir, I have always served France."[1] Napoleon tweaked Rapp's mustache and hired him back. Characteristic Rapp behavior perhaps, but any family connection with the Count is thrown into doubt by Isaac Hamilton Rapp's obituary reporting his ancestry as early New York (New Amsterdam) Dutch, even though "Rapp" is an archaic German word meaning black horse. In any event, Count Rapp would have been roughly contemporary with I. H.'s grandfather Alexander Hamilton Rapp whose parents were in New York when their son was born in 1808. These conflicting family accounts confirm that the Rapp architects, like many Americans, were never much concerned with foreign ancestry. Their habit was to look ahead.

The Rapps of more recent history than the Count never were military people by nature but were not exempt from having to live and work through times of war. Isaac was commissioned in 1862 as a Civil War second lieutenant, Company D, 81st Regiment, Illinois Volunteers, under Captain Cornelius S. Ward from Murphysboro. Before the war Isaac had given the captain's name to his son

Mason Gerardi Rapp in 1920 at New Mexico Military Institute. (Rapp Collection)

Hagerman Barracks at New Mexico Military Institute, designed by I. H. & W. M. Rapp in a castle style similar to the one their brother C. W. Rapp used in his Illinois school buildings. I. H. & W. M. Built the rest of NMMI's campus in the same scheme. Hagerman Barracks became Mason Rapp's home for four years. (Ken Fletcher Collection)

Cornelius Ward Rapp. As Captain Isaac Rapp he became a life member in the Union's Society of the Army of the Tennessee. By accident of age and history Isaac Hamilton, William Mason, C. W. and George Rapp never were called to the military. Their brother Lou's son, also named Louis, did become an army career officer who finished his service during World War II as commanding officer of the Presidio army base in San Francisco.

W. M. Rapp's son Mason, born in Trinidad, Colorado, in 1906, was too young for the first war and almost too old for the second, but served military time with four years as a high school cadet among the buildings his father and Uncle Ham had designed at Roswell's New Mexico Military Institute (NMMI). His mother's maiden name of Gerardi was Mase's middle name, and as M. G. Rapp he got the nickname "Machine Gun" after winning a string of marksmanship medals. He was awarded equestrian medals too, spending endless hours on horseback doing cavalry formation, gymkhanas and saber drills. Much attention was given to long marches; riding in a column of twos, muzzle to croup, and on command fanning out into a long line for classic cavalry charges at dummy saber targets. It was the duty of every NMMI cadet to feed and groom his own mount. As a holdover from the Mexican and Indian wars, training went on this way in this branch of the army until 1948, when at last the old remounts were retired to pasture and the horse cavalry disappeared into the armored divisions.

Beginning in 1920 Mase also spent three scorching summers with the cavalry at Fort Huachuca, Arizona, doing still more drill and dealing with cross-border bandits. These were followers of the revolutionary Pancho Villa who was still an abiding influence until he was assassinated in 1923. The climate and terrain were unforgiving. Cadets learned to empty their boots of scorpions every morning before putting them on and wrapping their puttee leggings. For Mason, those years defined the military as unpromising.

Mason Rapp's attempted picture perfect jump turned out to be less than that. Mason suffered bruises to his body and ego but nonetheless was an expert horseman at NMMI. (Rapp Collection)

Mason's cousin Louie Rapp, the son of I. H. and Will Rapp's brother Louis, was an upperclassman at NMMI when Mase entered as a freshman in 1920. Louis, his wife Martha and infant son came from Carbondale to Trinidad in 1903. He was not an architect but stayed close to the building trades. From Trinidad he moved with his family to Albuquerque in 1905 where he worked for Laughlin Hydro Stone Company. The expertise in finished lumber he gained from his father Isaac got him a position in 1907 with Herman & Cashman Lumber Company, also in Albuquerque. For his health he moved his family again, this time to Denver in 1910 where he was a representative for New Mexico Lumber Company. The high and dry climate didn't help and Louis Rapp, always called Lou, died from tuberculosis that same year in Denver's Oaks Home. He was remembered widely as affable and upright. His death meant that his young son Louie became like Mason a fatherless cadet at NMMI.

In 1920 shortly after Mason arrived at NMMI Louie distinguished himself by winning an oratory competition held at the University of New Mexico, Albuquerque. His speech on crime and prison reform was delivered reportedly "with force and ease." In 1921 he was named Honor Man and captain of NMMI's B Troop, graduating as a second lieutenant in the U. S. Army. He stayed-on at NMMI as an instructor. The school retained the old cavalry disciplinary practice of blows across the backside with a machine gun belt. Mason had this laid on more than once by Louie, whom Mase claimed did not hold back and appeared to enjoy it too much.

In the late 1930s Louie was stationed at Fort Sheridan north of Chicago. C. W. Rapp's widow Mary P. R. Rapp with Mason and his wife Virginia drove up for a visit, arriving about noon. Louie Rapp had always been a picture of the officer and gentleman; charismatic and sociable at gatherings and striking in his dress uniform. But when he came downstairs to greet his visitors in the reception room of the officers' quarters he was unshaven and reeking of alcohol. Without a word his Aunt Mary turned and left through the front door. Only the Army knew for sure but the suspicion was that Louie's drinking explained why, as an otherwise exemplary officer, he was never given battlefield command in WWII.

Military blood was thin in the Rapps but ran thick through the Brush side of the family, starting with Carbondale's General Daniel Harmon Brush in the Civil War. During that war parts of southern Illinois were so-called "copperhead country," a reference to pockets of southern sympathizers in northern border states. At a critical pre-war moment when local tempers were short, Brush declared himself by publicly raising the Union flag over his offices. This was a bold and potentially dangerous move that effectively calmed local disputes and coalesced Jackson County as a dependable Union bastion. In the first days of the war the North hardly had an army, and the number of recruits they could call up quickly often gave men rank. Brush used his influence to muster soldiers in a hurry, and for that was given a colonelcy. Later he was made general by brevet, an honorary increase in rank without a pay raise, and was addressed routinely for the rest of his life as General Brush.

D. H. Brush II as Brigadier General. He fought Indians in the American West, Spanish in Cuba and resistance in the Philippines. (Brush Collection)

The Rapp architects' sister Harriet's husband was General Brush's son D. H. Brush II, who was himself a soldier. In turn Harriet saw her son, Rapp & Rapp's Dan Brush, deploy for France during World War I as an officer in the 1st Division, 5th Field Artillery under Major (later colonel) Robert R. McCormick, the eccentric publisher of the Chicago Tribune. It was here that Dan met his future bride Evelyn Dumas, daughter of a Protestant minister, when her family provided simple kindness and French cooking for tired Yankee soldiers who came through her hometown of Saumur on the Loire southwest of Paris. Evelyn rejected the notion that she was a war bride, in that Dan did not bring her home from the war but returned afterwards to court her and propose marriage. News of his nephew's journey and engagement prompted only one comment from the preoccupied C. W. Rapp. "Well," said Rapp, "he went a long way."

Dan's father D.H. Brush II, West Point class of 1871, had set the military bar high for his son, with a long army career that he ended in 1912 as a brigadier general. As a 24-year-old second lieutenant in 1871 he was assigned to the 17th Infantry for duty at the Grand River Agency in Dakota, and in 1872 commanded a detachment of Indian scouts as part of the Yellowstone Expedition, engaging the Sioux in 1873 at the mouth of the Powder River in Montana. Many of Lieutenant Brush's troopers were foreigners who spoke no English but were promised citizenship in exchange for army service. Most were low born, rough and not very nice, but Brush was a well-trained disciplinarian who set high standards and expected compliance. His scouts routinely tracked Indians on foot for days and nights on end, and Brush worried about the health of his command. He ordered constant attention to personal cleanliness and routinely inspected for foot sores, often prescribing double layers of stockings and rubs of dry bar soap to prevent chafing.

In the same year of 1873 Brush II faced the Sioux again, this time at the fated Little Bighorn River, called Greasy Grass Creek by the Indians. Colonel George A. Custer once had commended Brush as one of his best scouts, which raises the question of what might have been had Brush been on hand with his scouting skills before the 7th Cavalry fell to the Sioux at the Little Bighorn in 1876.

With the nation urged on in 1898 by William Randolph Hearst's New York Journal and the slogan "Remember the Maine, to hell with Spain" after the U.S. battleship was sunk in Havana harbor, the States entered the Spanish-American War. Brush II went down to Cuba to fight in the Battle of El Caney and in engagements around Santiago. For gallantry at El Caney he got a silver star and was promoted to brevet major in 1898.

Daniel H. Brush I, II and III. The bearded Dan Brush was in the Civil War, D. H. II in the Spanish-American War, and number III in World War I. D. H. III was Rapp & Rapp's Dan Brush. (Brush Collection)

From the Spanish-American War the victorious U.S. inherited the Philippine Islands, and in 1899 Brush II was sent there, a place described in a report by Brush's commanding officer, Brigadier General J. F. Bell, in which "practically the entire population has been hostile to us at heart." Uprisings and insurgencies were widespread especially among the Moro tribesmen, mostly Sunni Muslims (the name "Moro" derived from the Spanish Moors) who had been raiding and waging guerilla warfare in the former Spanish colony off and on for 300 years. By 1904, as the inevitability and advantage of American protection clarified itself among most Filipinos, calm returned; and Colonel Brush was detailed to the Department of the Inspector General which administered the pacified islands. Harriet Rapp Brush joined her husband in the Philippines and set up house in a sweltering officers bungalow draped with mosquito netting. The two are buried together in Arlington National Cemetery.

At the same time their son, Rapp & Rapp's Dan Brush III, was studying for his civil engineering degree at the University of Illinois. Dan III's younger brother Major General Rapp Brush (his first name was his mother's maiden name) like his father, went to the Philippines, but under the very different conditions of World War II. In Panay and Luzon he served as commanding officer of the 40th Infantry Division under General Walter Kruger's Sixth Army, all under General Douglas MacArthur.

On the day following the Japanese attack on Pearl Harbor, the Wall Street Journal foretold the times ahead: "War with Japan means industrial revolution in the United States. The American productive machine will be reshaped with but one purpose—to produce the maximum of things needed to beat the enemy. It will be a brutal process." America became in effect a command economy with central planning all the way, which meant Mason Rapp, who in the 1930s gradually had taken over Rapp & Rapp office operation from his apathetic Uncle George, had his own war to fight, this one in Washington, D. C. with the War Production Board (WPB).

During World War II the WPB had the power to stop any job at any time; and while the war effort revived many businesses from the dead Depression years, architecture and construction were not among them. In Chicago, the skyline showed no new high-rise structures between the time of Graham, Anderson, Probst & White's art deco Field Building of 1934 to Naess & Murphy's modernist 1955 Prudential Building at Randolph and Michigan. The war effort stood first in line for materials. Projects deemed unnecessary by the WPB had to wait.

As oil is the blood of war, steel is its bone, which Mason Rapp was to discover in his own time as his uncles C.W. and George had in 1918 when they completed the State-Lake Building with reinforced concrete as steel disappeared into armaments. Twenty-four years later in 1942, Warner Brothers wanted to get more seats into Toledo, Ohio's Valentine Theatre in order to compete with the local Paramount on block booking (more seating meant first crack at first-run movies), and Rapp & Rapp was called. The Toledo Paramount that the Valentine competed against for patrons was a Rapp & Rapp from 1928, one of only two atmospheric-style theatres with characteristic sidewall parapets and open sky illusion turned out by the Rapp design department (the other was Chicago's Gateway Theatre in 1930).

Robert K. Bauerle, an architecture graduate and Kappa Sigma fraternity man from the University of Illinois, supervised the Valentine project. Mason hired the smart and personable Bauerle for his promise of selling more work for the office, but instead Bauerle moved with his wife into a Toledo apartment where he could watch over what turned out to be an increasingly trying project. Work on the Valentine began with McCarthy figuring on paper how best to add the most seating. The WPB was resistant from the start to a theatre project, but Rapp & Rapp proved instructive to other architects on how to win the Board's approval. They did it by pulling 120 tons of steel out of the old construction, cutting it free with acetylene-oxygen torches.

To shore up the job, Rapp & Rapp obtained construction columns left over from the Chicago subway, which Paschen Contractors had in storage. For the proscenium arch they used an economical combination of truss and plate girder. With sheet metal unavailable all the duct work was made of Transite, asbestos fused with cement under pressure to form an inert porcelain-like substance. Very tough and durable, the material was encouraged by the WPB because the government wanted to keep up employment in these related industries.

In addition to the subway columns another substitute for all the recaptured steel were timbers provided by Detroit Underpinning Company. The timbers had been set in place just at the moment Mason Rapp called from Chicago to report the WPB had stopped the job. With work on indefinite hold in the middle of a hot summer, humidity began to cause swelling in the timbers. Industrial fans were brought in to keep the set timbers as dry as possible, while Mason traveled to conference in Washington. Draftsmen spent a week of days and nights on site, redrawing portions of the project to achieve still more extraction of steel, a renewed effort that induced the Board to release the job. A new balcony girder proved they could achieve as much with less, and workmen extracted three additional tons of copper and steel.

There remained two decorative non-load-bearing columns on either side of the box office, about four feet in diameter, which had to come out to provide room for added patrons, but no one seemed clear on how to do it. Consensus was that the columns couldn't be removed without doing severe damage, until someone recalled a method used by the ancient Egyptians. Workers bored deep holes in the columns, drove in wedges and heated the wedges with torches. Expansion of the wedges caused the columns to part and peel like a banana. The segments weighed tons, but the columns were removed without harm to the structure.

Shortages of building materials created deprivations all across the home front, especially in housing which wound down to a near standstill as the war progressed. But before the war in 1940 nothing stood in the way of a man named Hubert Nelson who wanted to turn some of his Glenview, Illinois, nursery acreage into a housing development. His father Swain Nelson was known for having provided trees and shrubbery for landscape architect Frederick Law Olmsted's development of Jackson Park and the 1893 Chicago Columbian Exposition fairgrounds. The new housing development would be called Swainwood, and Hubert Nelson brought in Rapp & Rapp as architects.

Work was conceived in peacetime but progressed under the rumble of war planes training out of nearby Naval Air Station Glenview. Instead of bulldozing what was there, Nelson and Rapp & Rapp took seriously Olmsted's principles of naturalism by situating curved roadways, landscaping and houses amidst existing old growth trees. The clutter of overhead power lines was avoided with the first use of buried utilities. Mostly neo-classical in style, the homes were upscale and solidly built, each of a unique design. The idea of a housing development was new, and in its quality Swainwood remained uniquely separate from the mass postwar developments to come. A number of Swainwood homes were built early on, but war shortages slowed and finally stopped progress. By then the tone of the project had been set, and after the war it continued in phases with minimal Rapp & Rapp involvement.

In 1942 the office was also working on Ross Auditorium and Chapel for the Navy at Great Lakes Naval Training Center on Lake Michigan north of Chicago. Rapp & Rapp worked under Captain R. D. Spalding, public works officer headquartered at the Navy Yard in Portsmouth, New Hampshire. In April of the following year Mason began gathering his birth certificate, college transcripts and all the proper forms for a bid to join the Navy's construction battalion, called the Seabees. He calculated he would need a lieutenant commander's pay in order to support his home-front family. Spalding told Rapp the Navy didn't want architects as much as engineers, so to improve his bid Mason emphasized that aspect of his experience.

Rapp & Rapp's Ross Auditorium and Chapel. Built during World War II at Great Lakes Naval Training Center on the Lake Michigan shore north of Chicago, construction went on under strict wartime security. (Chicago History Museum)

Ross Auditorium's interior. (Chicago History Museum)

The Navy also wanted character references, one of whom was Justus Wilcox, secretary of the Libby Estate and head of Libby's Scott Properties, which owned Toledo's Valentine Theatre, and who had hired Rapp & Rapp for the Valentine renovation. Wilcox complied with Mason's reference request but separately challenged his reasoning. He pointed out Mason's advancing age, his current work with the Navy on Ross, his involvement in wartime housing with Swainwood and that he had a wife and three small children. Mason protested in a letter to Wilcox that he felt "very strongly that a man of my age should do something about the situation." In the end Mason dropped his application when Spalding presented essentially the objections Wilcox had posed. Without explanation Spalding added, "This war will be over soon anyway."

8 | "I AM A SIGMA CHI, SIR"

The sentiment of the old fraternity song, "I am a Sigma Chi, sir / Will be 'til I die, sir," ran through Rapp & Rapp starting with George, a Kappa Kappa chapter Sig at the University of Illinois, class of 1899. He was followed by his nephews Dan Brush ('06) and Ted Bullock ('09), both of whom were U. of I. Sigs. Dan's brother, Major General Rapp Brush, followed in the class of 1913. Mason Rapp ('29) came to Sigma Chi's Kappa Kappa chapter by a circuitous though destined way.

In May of 1920 when B. F. Keith's 105th Street Theatre in Cleveland was on C. W. & Geo. L. Rapp's drawing boards along with the Chicago and Tivoli, I. H. & W. M. Rapp were finishing Santa Fe's Pueblo Revival style La Fonda Hotel, the last building of many they had done together in New Mexico. At the same time a Trinidad doctor diagnosed Will's four-year-old younger son William Hamilton Rapp with polio. The doctor had seen the crippling disease among his troops during World War I. Without delay Mary Rapp packed her three children off to Los Angeles where Billy Ham could get the hospitalization and specialized treatment he needed. They stayed with Mary's brother Vince Gerardi and his family. Vince was an executive with the Italian Vineyards Company that became part of the vast Guasti winery. He had moved from Trinidad to California in 1898 carrying a letter of introduction from his father Pascal.

In Los Angeles Mason and his sister Mary Georgeina were sent to a local Catholic school where Mase resisted the religious rigor. Will Rapp quickly caught up on work and traveled to join his family. When he boarded the Santa Fe in Trinidad he was nursing a cold that worsened as he traveled west. By the time he got to Los Angeles he was weak with fever and unsteady on his feet.

His 14-year-old son Mason, dressed in Sunday clothes, raced down the platform to greet his dad. Will mussed his son's hair and said "Hi ya, Scrub," the last words Mason heard from his father. The

George Leslie Rapp as an architecture student at the University of Illinois. A member of the class of 1899, he was the first of four family architects initiated into Sigma Chi at U. of I. (University of Illinois Archives)

Grandmary Rapp after Will's death with Mason in his NMMI uniform, Mary Georgeina and William Hamilton who his father liked to call Billie Boy. (Rapp Collection)

family took Will home and put him to bed. He went to sleep and within hours died of pneumonia at age 57. Mary suddenly was a widow with a young son just afflicted with polio, and responsible alone for her other two children She was on her own as she was when her mother's death left her to care for Vince and sister Kate.

The loss affected Mason all his life, through which memories of his father were expressed only in isolated childhood glimpses. He remembered that Will liked to walk with him to Trinidad's rail yards to see the Santa Fe switch-on locomotives for the big pull west over the Rockies. Together they watched the strange and colorful Mexicans who came out of the mountains and from El Valle de los Rancheros to buy frijoles and material for clothing. At other times they watched doleful processions of the religious Penitentes pass along the banks of the Purgatory River. Mason also remembered chasing harmless snakes called puff adders that popped up through the board sidewalks of Fairhope, Alabama, where his father took him fishing in summers. Fairhope was a new progressive real estate development founded by the Fairhope Industrial Association, which intrigued Will Rapp as much as the fishing. Will didn't take many traveling vacations and was known to grumble about I. H. Rapp's frequent jaunts away from work to enjoy Dr. Kellogg's spa in Battle Creek, Michigan.

Will's work-related travel did keep him away for long periods but he always stayed engaged as a parent with frequent letters. In one written to Mason when the family was in Los Angeles with the Gerardis, Will apologized for having missed Mase's birthday. "I have a lot of work on hand, and when a fellow leaves his work for pleasure he isn't much of a fellow and not fit to be daddy for a good bunch of kids like I have." Will was always positive and upbeat. To him, and to many of his generation, negativity or defeatism was unmanly. He always encouraged Mason to keep up with his swimming and especially his music. In a letter written only months before he died, Will referred to the office draftsman A. C. Hendrickson when he wrote, "Mr. Hendrickson said this morning that he wanted you to come with him and work. He thinks you will make a draftsman if you will try. If you decide to take up the architectural profession, Mr. Hendrickson would help you more than anyone." Will always advised his son to be "square" with people, and once when Mason bought candy with money given to him for the Sunday collection box his father made him pay back the church in person.

In 1919 W. M. Rapp had become chairman of a forward-looking company called Home Builders, Inc., made up of local Trinidad businessmen. To get things started he worked without pay to design five modern 5-room homes in the California bungalow style. With Rapp on board, Home Builder's beginning was robust, but the company quickly lost direction and fell apart after Rapp's death in the early morning of June 4, 1920. That evening the Santa Fe and Trinidad newspapers bannered stories about who among a dozen possible candidates, including former president Taft, Major General Leonard Wood and Calvin Coolidge, would win the Republican nomination at the upcoming Chicago convention. In the midst of the politics were Will Rapp's respectful front-page obituaries praising his civic and architectural contributions to the Southwest.

Will left behind investments in stock and property, including the Walsenburg coal land, downtown Trinidad's Turner Building, White Front commercial block and the McCormick Building, in all of which his brother C.W. back in Chicago still held an interest. All this had to be sorted out by Rapp's co-executors; architectural partner A. C. Hendrickson and the trusted Frank Clements, Will's sister Annie's husband in Carbondale. William Mason Rapp was buried in Los Angeles' Hollywood Cemetery, close to what would become the Paramount movie lot. This was an irony for a man whose brothers in Chicago were about to have so much to do with spreading Hollywood and especially Paramount movies across the nation. More ironic still was that Will's quiet resting place would in the next few years become crowded by the graves of cinema legends and pioneers like the Chicago Rapps' client Jesse Lasky of Famous Players-Lasky, Cecil B. De Mille and numerous actors including Rudolph Valentino, whose reflecting pool dwarfed them all.

Less than a year following Rapp's passing came the equally sudden death of the office's Arthur Hendrickson, which left Hamilton Rapp as the sole surviving partner. With Hendrickson gone, Frank Clements in Carbondale became Will Rapp's absentee executor. Clements and the court agreed that this was impractical. He resigned and Mary Gerardi Rapp, who best knew her family's needs, was named executrix.

The office went on under I. H. Rapp with Francis W. Spencer, who had come with the Rapps in 1909, as chief draftsman. Newcomer Roy Voorhees became superintendent of construction. Will Rapp hired Voorhees from Raton in May 1920, only a month before Will died. Ham had been living in Santa Fe and returned to Trinidad to run the firm. Mary Rapp, Mason, Mary Georgeina and Billy Ham were on their own.

Mary, known to the next generation of family as Grandmary, faced pressing decisions after the death of her husband. In the summer of 1921 she worked in Trinidad's McCormick Building as a stenographer for Mutual Life Insurance Company's district manager P. N. Pattison. In September of that year she returned to Los Angeles where she enrolled daughter Mary G. in The Cumnock School, a boarding school for girls, while eldest son Mason went to the New Mexico Military Institute (NMMI) in Roswell. She reasoned that these arrangements gave her more time to deal with Will's estate and Billy Ham's therapy, but Mason at 14 and Mary at 12 felt isolated. Young Bill's care was uppermost in Grandmary's mind, and in January 1923 she moved to Denver, continuing her pursuit of the best polio specialists. In June the

Mase at New Mexico Military Institute. (Rapp Collection)

following year she and Bill met Mason and Mary G. in Trinidad and went back to Denver to spend the summer. In September 1924, Mary G. was sent to Monticello School for girls in Godfrey, Illinois, while Mason went back to Roswell. In May the following year Grandmary took Billy on a six month trip to Washington, D.C., still in search of the best medical care.

When Mason first enrolled at NMMI as a boy of 14 in 1920, he found himself alone and haunted among the Scottish baronial NMMI structures designed by his father and Uncle Ham. NMMI opened in 1898 with its earliest buildings designed by a local Roswell architect. In 1908 the NMMI Board of Regents contracted I. H. & W. M. Rapp to provide a master plan and specifications for a modern buildings and grounds plan. Hagerman Barracks was the first building of many to follow. The Rapp firm continued as NMMI's sole architect until completion of the President's House in 1931. Campus structures built since have developed modern variations on the Rapps' Collegiate/ Military Gothic style.

When Mason Rapp moved into Hagerman Barracks, he was homesick and lost in mourning for his father, who had only recently given him a little flute-like instrument. Mase played the instrument into those first nights after lights out. This was against regulations but the commanding officer knew the boy's situation and let it happen. Roswell students lived by the bugle, and when Taps sounded every night Mason silently mouthed his own words to each phrase: "Be a man / Be a man..." It was the kind of thing his father would have said to him.

Into the military routine, Mason saw none of his family except for his Uncle Ham who came down to Roswell once a month to take him out for a haircut. Ham had other business there too, still advancing NMMI's building program and working on various Roswell residences. The next four years for Mason amounted to winters at NMMI and summers with the cavalry near the Mexican border at Fort Huachuca. From Trinidad's Rice School, added to in 1889 by Uncle Ham, Mase had gone on to the Rapp-designed NMMI campus whose architectural scheme was patterned after C. W. Rapp's Collegiate Gothic designs of the 1890s. Four years later, he again found himself under the distant shadow of his family, this time in the Sigma Chi Kappa Kappa chapter house at the University of

Rapp & Rapp's Kappa Kappa chapter Sigma Chi house built at the university of Illinois in 1909 and reproduced here from a 1938 photograph. (Sigma Chi Fraternity)

First rendering in 1910 of C. W. & Geo. L. Rapp's Alpha chapter house for Sigma Chi at Miami of Ohio. The front portico was left out of the final design. (Sigma Chi Fraternity)

The final Alpha House design built by Rapp & Rapp in 1913. (Sigma Chi Fraternity)

Illinois. Mason's uncles Ward and George had designed that Tudor-style house in 1909.

Local Greek letter designations like Kappa Kappa denote the order in which a chapter was chartered, starting with Alpha, then Alpha Beta and on through the alphabet. Sigma Chi's founding Alpha Chapter was chartered in 1855 at Miami University in Oxford, Ohio. U. of I.'s Kappa Kappa followed far on in order. One of two famous literary Sigs from Purdue (the other was Booth Tarkington, class of 1893, who wrote The Magnificent Ambersons) was George Ade, 1887, who produced a creed for Sigma Chi, which began, "I believe in fairness, decency and good manners." These few words encapsulated the general ideal of the college fraternities that sprouted in the 19th century as a Midwest answer to eastern Ivy League eating clubs.

Idealistic sentiments in fact played a part in Sigma Chi's 1855 founding when the Delta Kappa Epsilon ("Deke") chapter at Miami of Ohio was ready to vote for a chapter poet. Four members in good conscience refused to vote for the slated candidate because to them he lacked "poetic abilities," and out of this schism the breakaway four with two others founded Sigma Chi's Alpha Chapter. A half century later the fraternity wanted a memorial to the charter members, and by general subscription financed The Founders' Memorial Chapter House, a large Georgian home for the "Mother Chapter" in Oxford, Ohio. The property title was in the name of the Grand Council of the Sigma Chi Fraternity and the building architects were C. W. & Geo. L. Rapp of Chicago. Employing a mistake-proof method often used by their father, Rapp & Rapp took the extra step of drawing foldout templates in actual size for carpenters to use on site when milling lumber for the sideboards and fireplace mantles. With all this heavy heritage behind him, Mason Rapp was destined for two things when he got to the

University of Illinois in 1924—to attend the school of architecture and to pin on his lapel the Sigma Chi Norman Shield and White Cross of Constantine.

Fraternity recruitment, called rushing, was more aggressive in those times than the deferred rush of today. No more is there a tactic called sandbagging, which meant securing a worthy candidate before he ever got to campus or knew of other possibilities. The Kappa Kappa brothers reviewed records of incoming freshmen and sent emissaries up to Chicago on the Illinois Central to nab any selected prey as he arrived on the station platform, usually accompanied by his parents. The method was to jolly the neophyte along, take him in tow aboard the train and, using pressure and flattery in a party atmosphere, have a pledge pin on him before they got south of Kankakee. Mason, preceded by letters of recommendation from his Sig cousins and prominent Sigma Chi Uncle George, was a sure "legacy" with no alternative.

Fraternities provided young men with a home away from home, and with alumni backing could offer better room and board than university housing. To move the pledges along, older fraternity brothers were charged with counseling, prodding and tutoring, instilling positive study habits, getting the reluctant involved, finding dates for the shy or teaching table manners and social graces to farm boy freshmen. Mason benefited from this spirit and never forgot it. While things are different on the Roswell campus today, Mason's problem was four years of sporadic and poor preparation at NMMI, where many instructors were ailing army officers assigned to New Mexico for health reasons rather than teaching ability. The smell of tobacco-free Cubeb cigarettes, purportedly good

The Sigma Chi chapter at the University of Illinois gathered on the fraternity house lawn for this 1927 photo. Mason Rapp, second from right in the top row, was chapter Consul (president) that year. The fraternity house in the background was designed in 1909 by his uncles C. W. and Geo. L. Rapp. (Rapp Collection)

for asthma, was constant. Not all the instructors were ineffec-
tual. One math teacher, whose chief attribute appears to have
been patience, seemed to have eyes in the back of his head. In
fact he watched the class from the blackboard by reflections from
his eyeglasses. He could single out restless individuals for questions without facing the class, and if a cadet failed to rise while
giving his answer the instructor, without looking from the blackboard, would say, "Stand at attention." His signature response
to any failed answer was, "Wrong! Erroneous! Not right!" This
conscientious instructor notwithstanding, Mason missed many
fundamentals of secondary school and had to spend a remedial
year in University High School before he could begin as a college freshman. His fraternity brothers grasped the problem and
pushed him hard by nagging, drilling and structuring his study.
The brothers could be overbearing and obnoxious, but without
them, Mason later acknowledged, he never would have made it.
In many ways Sigma Chi replaced the support that went missing
when Mason lost his father.

During summer breaks, Mase joined the sea of draftsmen and
designers that flooded Rapp & Rapp's Chicago office during the
1920s. He was assigned to fill-in poché and do other tedious work
that designers liked to avoid. His Uncle Ward (C.W.) treated him
no better or worse than anyone else as he made his daily 11 a.m.
descent from his office to the drafting room and passed like a professor among the tables. Pausing with a nod when he got to Mase,
he might offer minimal comments like "Good" or "You might
think that over." Mason and Ward got a first impression of each
other in 1924, when Mase arrived on the Santa Fe from Colorado
the summer before he started at the University of Illinois. George
Rapp was supposed to meet him at the station but failed to arrive.
Mase called his Aunt Mary who paid for his taxi to her south side
apartment. He was wearing a rumpled green suit he'd outgrown
when he met his Uncle, who looked his nephew up and down
and said to Mary, "Get the boy a hat."

At the Sigma Chi house there was the usual hazing, paddling and
partying, but these traditions mostly were contained. Gentlemanly
sportsmanship was held in high regard. It was a more mannerly
time. Drunkenness, foul language in company, date rape, van-
dalism and the like were not even concepts. Contentious gender
issues had no place. Even in the middle of the Roaring 20s,
alcohol consumption was almost nil among the clueless college
generation that danced the Charleston, Black Bottom and Varsity

College Picture of Mason
Rapp outside the University of
Illinois' architecture building,
Champaign, Illinois, probably
taken at graduation, 1929. (Rapp
Collection)

University Hall on the quiet idyllic U. of I. campus in the late 1920s when Mason Rapp was a student. (Rapp Collection)

Pencil sketch of Mason Rapp done by an architecture school classmate. (Rapp Collection)

Drag, though all the talk of Prohibition tempted a few Sigs to try their hand at making beer. No one was brave enough to sample it, so the brothers stored the brew in the Sig house attic. After a few hot days the bottles bubbled over and destroyed the ceiling below. All this had to be explained to alumni who bore the cost of repair.

The reality of social life was in fact very tame, consisting mainly of attending sorority tea dances on invitation and hosting fraternity formals. For the Kappa Kappa Sigs the formal dances were unusually grand, thanks in large part to a piano-playing Phi Delt named Bill Goodheart who as an undergraduate had developed a profitable band-booking business. Through Goodheart the Kappa Kappa formals benefited from the best jazz available in an age named for jazz. Goodheart later with Jules Stein formed Music Corporation of America, the latter-day MCA. Other aspects of social life included movie dates at the Orph (Champaign's Rapp & Rapp Orpheum Theatre) followed by ice cream sodas. Stylish co-eds bobbed their hair, talked about their beaus and wore raccoon coats with the open flapping galoshes that got the girls known as flappers. The hot music and full dance cards on campus created in the wider population a culture centered on the mystique of youth and college life, reflected in the movies and books of the time. Most captivating was Big Ten football, largely because of the University of Illinois' nationally famous gridiron hero Red Grange, and the new half-time persona Chief Illiniwek, a war-dancing symbol of courage on the football field.

One great social and financial friend of Sigma Chi in Champaign was an aging lady and good sport known as Gram Trevitt, heiress of a local banking family. Gram was young at heart and once said to Mason's girl Virginia, "Ginna, I'm getting old and I hate it!" If you were among a select few couples, Gram would have you to semi-formal dinners in her stately home set amidst old elms. The evenings might include a sample of bootlegged scotch but that was all the drinking there was. Only the wealthiest few students on the tree-lined campus had cars, the occasional Cord or Stutz, so that was a social problem for the future. It was all very tame indeed, and very innocent.

Mason Rapp's instruction at the University of Illinois' School of Architecture and Kindred Subjects followed the beau ideal of Ecole des Beaux-Arts in Paris; as had the schooling of every other formally trained architect in the Western World since the institution was founded in 1671 at the command of King Louis XIV. The man who codified the Beaux-Arts method for the modern world in his *Elements et theories de l'architecture* of 1902 was Julien Gaudet (1834–1908). He stressed integrity of construction, skillful drawing and mastery of detail. According to Beaux-Arts method the orders of architecture (i.e. windows, doors, pediments, entablatures, et al) are developed around the main axis (centerline) drawn vertically through a plan. Using the centerline as an anchor, order and balance are maintained as the plan develops outward from it. As Gaudet put it, "Our art is an heir rich with the accumulated legacies of the centuries; its invariable principle is reason, logic, method... the classic is not the privilege of any time, country or school... its principles are the same in all artistic ages, in spite of differences in exterior forms."[1] Part of the Beaux Arts method was to impress with ever-increasing spectacle—in the case of Rapp & Rapp theatres the visitor is greeted with an elegant ticket lobby leading to an impressive grand lobby and finally into a spectacular main house. The cumulative effect was designed to be breathtaking.

The formal rules of order and tradition developed under the Beaux-Arts method continued supreme up to World War II; applied in its purest way in America by architects like McKim, Mead & White and Paul Cret. I. H. & W. M. Rapp used the methods in designing Santa Fe's Territorial Capitol (1896) and Trinidad's Las Animas County Court House (1916). C. W. Rapp applied Beaux-Arts principles in his college and court house architecture, and Chicago's Rapp & Rapp developed all their big theatres that way, modified according to movie palace requirements and often simplified to speed the job. In America the influential Beaux-Arts Institute of Design was founded by Lloyd Warren (1869–1922) whose coveted Medal of Honor went one year to Arthur F. Adams, his ticket into the Ecole des Beaux-Arts, capture of the Paris Prize and eventual move to C. W. & Geo. L. Rapp in 1921.

Mason never claimed to have the remarkable drawing skills of Adams and his fellow Beaux-Arts scholars, but his training was essentially the same, filled with order and rigor. Always around the corner was another "esquisse," a sketch drill that took nine hours "en loge," meaning alone in a cubicle with nothing but pencils and paper. The idea was to present a rough sketch at 1/8-inch scale of a "parti" or scheme, whose specifications were revealed by the instructor only just before the student cloistered himself. Minimal bathroom breaks were allowed but none for food. Isolation was intended to plumb the depths of a student's knowledge without group influence. The esquisse required plan, elevation and section, i.e. views from above, front and side. Other drills stressed dimensional and relief rendering in various scales, achieved by striking shadows as they would fall before a light source from a given level and direction. Lettering, inking and watercolor handling came on the way to the "analytique," the final exam. The idea behind all this rigor was to instill mastery of architectural order, proportion and consistency.

Sigma Chi helped Mason get through all this, as the fraternity had done for George Rapp years before. It also provided the local connections George needed to get the Champaign Orpheum job for Rapp & Rapp (1914), which closely followed the work on Miami of Ohio's Alpha Memorial house. In years to come Mason revisited his uncles' Tudor style Kappa Kappa chapter house with 1950s alterations, and he designed changes for the Sigma Chi national headquarters in Evanston, Illinois. Sigma Chi's later new Evanston national headquarters might have gone to Rapp & Rapp but was lost to another architect, leaving Mason with the sting of insult. Rapp & Rapp's most faithful Sigma Chi client was Carl P. Clare. He owned an electrical component manufacturing firm that carried his name. As an early example of a building intended for what would come to be known as high tech manufacture, Rapp & Rapp's modernist Clare plant of 1952 and 1958 would seem the stuff of science fiction.

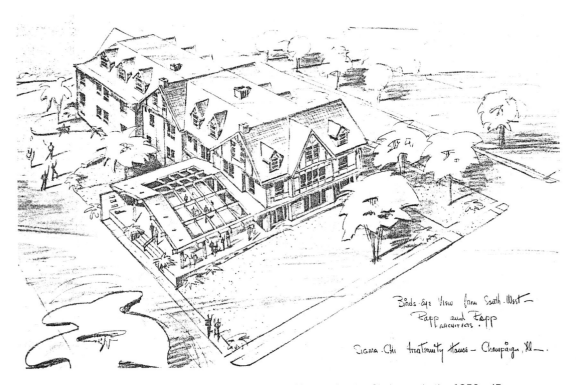

Modernizations by Rapp & Rapp provided for the Kappa Kappa chapter Sig house in the 1950s. (Rapp Collection)

9 | PROHIBITION

The years in America when the manufacture, sale and transport of liquor were illegal paralleled the movie palace golden age almost exactly, from the world's first real movie palace, Rapp & Rapp's Central Park (1917) for Balaban & Katz, to New York's Radio City Music Hall (1932), for which the Rapp office was technical consultant to the Rockefellers' architects. Congress ratified prohibition in January 1919, just two months after the World War I armistice. Progressives like Frances Willard's Woman's Christian Temperance Union (WCTU), who deplored the laboring classes spending their pay in saloons, had worked to pass the ban while troops were overseas fighting the war. The veterans returned to a different America from the one they had left to defend.

Always there are those who work to improve the world by controlling the behavior of everyone else. In this regard the Prohibitionists were exemplary. Mainly rooted in a Protestant ethic tinged with anti-foreign concern (beer was German, wine was Italian), Prohibition reflected this tendency to cleanse and purify through intolerance. Mark Twain reacted against previous anti-saloon efforts with sardonic humor, writers like Fitzgerald and Hemingway after World War I opposed it by living in France where they could get a legal drink, and George Rapp resisted in his own small way by building a lodge in the wilds of northern Wisconsin far from the teetotaling crowd. Rapp was no wooly outdoorsman and certainly no hunter, fisherman or backpacker, but he was one of the many who flouted Prohibition by lifting a glass for liberty. Even before Prohibition became law many people opposed the ever-present principle with laughter, the only weapon they had – both George Rapp and Dan Brush in their turn received Sigma Chi's satirical "WCTU Award."

Prohibition was a thirteen year social experiment implemented by the Volstead Act, the eighteenth amendment to the U.S. Constitution, which succeeded in creating a legendary criminal class of bootleggers and was mourned by few after repeal. When repeal did come in 1933, as one of President Franklin D. Roosevelt's first official acts, drinking was not only permitted but became a sort of patriotic obligation for many who might not otherwise have touched a drop.

In 1931, after Prohibition had been the law of the land for more than a decade, George Rapp happened to pick up a book of nostalgia titled Old Waldorf Bar Days by a New York journalist named Albert Stevens Crockett. No doubt George related to the book's idealistic dedication, which read:

"In memory of certain gentlemen of other days, who made of drinking one of the pleasures of life - not one of its evils; who achieved content long ere capacity was reached or overtaxed; and who, whatever they drank, proved able to carry it, keep their heads and remain gentlemen, even in their cups."

The book listed hundreds of drink recipes (with names like Gloom Lifter, Goat's Delight and Stone Fence), many of which were named after regulars at the long lost Brass Rail Bar of the old Waldorf. George also kept a copy of Harry Johnson's New and Improved Bartenders' Manual from 1900 that listed still other exotic drink recipes, along with imposing instructions on how bartenders were supposed to behave and serve. George remained uninfluenced by all the described drink mixtures and stayed mostly with scotch whiskey highballs, or as close to scotch as he could find during the dry years.

George Rapp's regular late afternoon cocktail session in his office was not the antisocial exercise it may seem. Without legal public bars, civilized pre-dinner cocktails were privately ritualized in the 1920s and flourished openly after repeal. Roosevelt liked his martinis, and for all we know even he quietly ignored the law during Prohibition. In its pure form the American institution called the cocktail hour was a time set aside to relax, converse or simply contemplate. The problem was that the ritual could get out of hand. Because Prohibition had been such a stiff regime, drunkenness became socially tolerated, the butt of good comedy and even admired among the faster crowds. Ideally, however, being able to hold your liquor like ladies and gentlemen was as important as the right to have it in the first place.

C. W. and Mary P. R. Rapp were among those especially annoyed by Prohibition. They were adults of advancing age who always

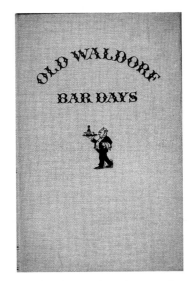

Cover of George Rapp's copy of Old Waldorf Bar Days, a book he bought in 1931 for its nostalgia. (Rapp Collection)

George Rapp also kept a copy of Harry Johnson's manual. This illustration shows how bartenders were expected to behave in 1888. (Rapp Collection)

enjoyed their martini each evening and were not happy about suddenly being put on the wrong side of the law. They were true believers in self-policing temperance, not the enforced abstinence of the WCTU, and they found quiet ways through discreet purveyors with foreign sources to obtain their Gordon's gin and Martini & Rossi vermouth. George Rapp had bootleggers too who regularly delivered whiskey to his office. Sometimes the quality of the product appeared suspect, and George would send the office's man-of-all-trades Peter Hoffman over to a downtown lab to have samples tested for impurities. Hoffman was a handy generalist who worked as needed on everything from messenger service to job supervision. Though no architect, he knew construction and was even sent to oversee the Denver Orpheum job. He came to Rapp & Rapp from Marshall & Fox architects when C. W. hired him in an impromptu sidewalk interview outside the State-Lake Building.

George kept his bottles in a cabinet in C. W.'s office and, after hours every day, broke them out and set up in his own office. He had willing drinking friends, most regularly Ernie Lieberman from Lieberman, Klein & Hein, the structural engineers Rapp & Rapp used on the big theatres, and whose offices were downstairs from the Rapps in the State-Lake building. Because of his unpredictable petit-mal epilepsy George never let himself drive and instead was chauffeured in his Cunningham by a black man named Robert. Robert kept the automobile washed, serviced and tightly locked away like the crown jewels in a nearby garage. Robert with his wife Adelaide kept up George's Windermere West apartment. He cooked and shopped for groceries at Stop & Shop's downtown store while she did the housework and fed George's aloof cat Maggie. Robert liked to do things his own way at his own pace, prompting George to speak of him as Sir Robert.

Part of Robert's job was to drive George to the office every morning and pick him up in the evenings. At 6 p. m. he would wheel-up in the Cunningham and park on State Street near Wacker Drive, in view of the State Lake building. When cocktails were finished, George would open the office window overlooking State Street and broadly wave his arm, and Robert would have the car down in front by the time George got there. It became a way of life and, despite the bother of Prohibition, business at the office boomed and work went on.

One afternoon in 1922 George's secretary Veronica Walsh put through a long distance call from New York. On the line was Adolph Zukor, president of Famous Players-Lasky, predecessor of Paramount Pictures. He had seen Balaban & Katz's Chicago and Tivoli theatres, and others Rapp & Rapp built for B. F. Keith, which became RKO (Radio Keith Orpheum), and he wanted something like that in New York. George responded by packing his Gladstone bag and boarding the New York Central at La Salle Street Station.

Tracing the corporate twists and turns of the movie business can be complicated, but for Paramount under Zukor it went from Famous Players to Famous Players-Lasky with Jesse Lasky, to Paramount-Publix, and to Paramount Pictures until 1936. At that point, with the studio in financial trouble, Zukor was kicked upstairs as chairman and Paramount was rescued by its new president Barney Balaban from Chicago. Even by 1926 Paramount in effect had become a practical extension of Balaban &Katz, which accounted for so much of the Paramount work done by Rapp & Rapp. In the 1950s the company was turned over to Balaban's hand-picked successor Leonard Goldenson and became ABC-Paramount. Today it is a subsidiary of Viacom run by Sumner Redstone. Zukor's memorable contribution to the nascent industry was to combine film production, distribution and exhibition under one corporate umbrella, an arrangement that came to be called the studio system. Paramount, and soon other companies, made its own films for distribution to its own nation-wide network of theatres, and this is where Rapp & Rapp came in.

Zukor in 1922 secured a choice piece of property on Broadway at Times Square that held the Putnam Building, named for Revolutionary War general Israel Putnam.[1] The general was most remembered for his command at the Battle of Bunker Hill, "Don't fire 'til you see the whites of their eyes." In a prime example of one generation tearing down the icons of the previous, Zukor wanted the property used for a Paramount headquarters building including the best theatre money could buy. The Putnam building would go, and no effort in replacing it was to be spared. It seemed like Balaban & Katz revisited, but Zukor was no Barney Balaban. When it came to the architects' six percent fee he balked where Balaban would have had no argument. George stood firm and left New York empty handed.

When he got back to the office Miss Walsh handed him a waiting telegram from Zukor. Six percent would be fine. Once again George followed the red carpet leading passengers to the Twentieth Century Limited bound for New York, signed the contracts and came home again. The relationship between Rapp & Rapp and Zukor's Paramount led to many more Rapp theatres bearing Paramount's famous mountain logo, in styles ranging from C. W. Rapp's favored Second Empire French through the Toledo Paramount's atmospheric treatment to the Aurora, Illinois, Paramount of 1931 done in what the Rapp office called Paris Fair style. Abbreviated as Art Deco today, Paris Fair style referred to the modern design developed at the Exposition Internationale des Arts Decoratifs et Industriels Modernes of 1925. At about the same time, the firm used a similar high Deco treatment for the Denver Orpheum.

Zukor had a wise second thought when he hired Rapp & Rapp for the Times Square Paramount, proved by the finished product opened in 1926: a gorgeous, modern 25-story office skyscraper with Art Deco setbacks, topped with a clock tower visible for miles. The building was located in the heart of the Great White Way, the most glamorous acreage in the world. Broadway, teeming with life and bathed in the light of theatre marquees, presented an unequaled spectacle. First among the unequaled was the Paramount marquee, a graceful piece of industrial design drawn in a soft arch that became Rapp & Rapp's signature "French curve." The grand lobby design drew heavily on the

CONSTRUCTION OF PARAMOUNT BUILDING
TIMES SQUARE - NEW YORK CITY →1926

Paramount Building going up in 1926 at Times Square, New York City. To the right is the Astor Hotel where Rapp & Rapp rented rooms for offices during construction. (Rapp Collection)

Office rendering of the New York City Paramount Building. (Art. Adams Collection)

Period depiction of Charles Garnier's Paris Opera grand lobby which influenced the Rapps' treatment of Paramount Theatre. (Rapp Collection)

Paramount grand stairway, very much in the Paris Opera spirit. (Rapp Collection)

Ad for the Times Square Paramount from September 25, 1926. (Art. Adams Collection)

Adolph Zukor, president of Famous Players-Lasky, was so proud of his Paramount that he had his image superimposed over the building's. This mock-up apparently was never used. (Art. Adams Collection)

Ongoing competition for patrons began outside with ever larger and more powerful theatre marquees. The muscular but graceful deco Paramount marquee defined a Rapp & Rapp design characteristic called the "French Curve." (Rapp Collection)

Paris Opera, except that it was larger than Garnier's work in order to accommodate huge crowds of movie house patrons.

The Paramount opening was a well-publicized event and the public loved it, but Rapp & Rapp always had detractors among certain sophisticates. Proto-Bauhaus avant-gardes thought the architecture retrograde, and other purists objected to applying Beaux-Arts principles to anything so common as movie theatres. While negative critics uniformly praised the engineering involved in movie palace architecture, they quibbled about the use of ornamental plaster where marble might have been; and it seemed somehow vulgar that the buildings could go from drafting board to opening night in just a year. Clever people among the smart set referred to anything that looked overly decorated as too "Balaban & Katzy."

Architect Thomas Tallmadge wrote in Exhibitors Herald and Moving Picture World: "No more pitiful degradation of an art has ever been presented than the prostitution of architecture that goes on daily in the construction of these (movie palace) buildings. If art suffers, what of the minds of the youngsters who see about them taste and beauty abased to the lowest degree." The New Yorker in November 1926 wrote that the Paramount Building "is the sort of design which is likely to knock the layman for a loop while leaving the instructed critic more than cold... The step-backs [sic] of the Broadway elevation are dispiritingly monotonous, a dreary series of steps in which nothing predominates." Elsewhere in The New Yorker: "With the help of the most advanced engineering skill the building rears itself as an architectural insult to one's sense of stability."[2] Asked his opinion by a reporter after all this criticism George Rapp only quipped, "Harry Thaw shot the wrong architect," referring to the Pittsburgh millionaire playboy who a few years before had killed Stanford White in a scandalous love triangle. During the years of the Paramount planning and construction Rapp & Rapp rented rooms on the fifth floor of the neighboring Astor Hotel. C.W.'s architect nephew, sister Annie's son Edwin C. A. (Ted) Bullock managed this superintending office. All design work was done, as always, in the Chicago office under the eye of C. W. Ted closed up the spare room he occupied in George's Windermere West apartment, moved to New York and never came back.

When the Paramount job was well enough along, Rapp & Rapp moved from the Astor into permanent offices in the new building. The idea was to generate and supervise more East Coast work. C. W. put Ted in charge. In came more contracts, including the Brooklyn Paramount at DeBevoise and DeKalb Streets. The New York office also brought in two of Marcus Loew's "Wonder Theatres," the massive Kings also in Brooklyn at Flatbush and Tilden, and the Jersey in Jersey City. During this heady time the handsome and outgoing Bullock found his new wife Rita, a New York executive secretary. They loved the city with all its shops and street vendors, the seductive romance of Broadway night life, Ted's status as a superstar architect and their showplace penthouse apartment with its outdoor garden. George Rapp thought Ted, whom he called "the blond," had gone too far in his enthusiasm for the Big Apple, an apparently incurable condition George called "New Yawkitis." George often expressed his reverse snobbery this way. When family members began to move from Chicago's south side to the north shore, George said they had deserted him for the "nawth shaw." Always suspicious of architectural theorizing, George deemed overly intellectualized architecture as a product of the Harvard school, dismissively pronounced as "hahvud."

Definitely not hahvud was Chicago's Oriental Theatre, a 1926 design phantasy built for Balaban & Katz. A big change from C. W.'s favored French elegance, the Oriental was a masterpiece of free-for-all entertainment architecture and a tour-de-force from Arthur Adams' design department. Adams' men plowed through George's office library, gathering from the volumes any motif that appeared appropriately exotic. For the fantastic interior ornament Adams hired a sculptor named Arthur Büttner (who pronounced his name as BYEWTner). He arrived off the street carrying samples of his work in his pockets. Adams liked what he saw and asked the man when he could start. Bütner said he would need a day or two to find an apartment. He had left his wife and child on a park bench where they were living. Büttner went to work creating casts for the plaster elephants, dragons and Hindu gods that made the interior appear more of the Indian subcontinent than the Orient in general. Nothing like it had ever been done, and Dan Brush was responsible for carefully supervising application of ornamental detail on-site and through the photographs that crossed his desk daily.

Oriental Theatre view toward sidewall and organ screen. (Chicago History Museum)

Two opposing legends exist about the birth of the Oriental. One was that Rapp & Rapp shocked the Balabans with the result, and the other that the Balabans forced the Rapps into it. Both versions have some truth, at least according to Mason Rapp, who said Barney Balaban liked the French approach but wanted something "different." C. W. agreed and Adams was unleashed. Balaban was surprised at the developing scheme and, according to Adams, needed some encouragement; but he liked that it made people smile in addition to inspiring awe. The story that C. W. and George voted disapproval of their own work by refusing to attend opening night is unconfirmed. The anecdote implies that C. W. was a prisoner of his aggressive army of designers, which never was the case.

The office skyscraper housing the Oriental was done for the Masonic Order in a design more straightforward than the treatment for the theatre interior. Balaban & Katz leased the theatre space from the Masons, whose construction representatives insisted on additional and separate structural support for the office building in case the theatre failed financially and had to be torn out. After the Oriental's opening in May 1926, it was plain that the owners needn't have worried. The ultimate architecture critics, the ticket-buying public, made the Oriental an instant and ongoing success.

Earlier office rendering of C. W. & Geo. L. Rapp's Masonic building was changed for the final design (Art. Adams Collection)

Plaster ornament above Chicago's Oriental Theatre proscenium (Chicago History Museum)

Ceiling detail in the Oriental. (Chicago History Museum)

Many miles away and a week before the Times Square Paramount opened on November 19, 1926, the following unrelated item appeared in the Mellen, Wisconsin, Weekly-Record: "The first sleighs of the winter were seen on Mellen streets Tuesday morning. N. W. Fochs made a trip to Mineral Lake with a load of supplies for the Rapp Brothers' building crew, on sleighs." George Rapp's lodge was taking shape.

The Weekly-Record story was only partly right. By that November there was only one Rapp brother. C. W. had died of a massive stroke the previous June. His wife Mary's nephew Franklin Brewer happened to be visiting. He helped the attending doctor cool Rapp's face with damp cloths and turn him in bed through the night. With nothing more to be done in what amounted to a death watch, Rapp was gone by the morning of June 28, at age 66.

There had been no warning, and the shock was wide and deep. Adams got the word and announced C.W.'s death to work crews from the stage of the St. Louis Ambassador Theatre where he was supervising construction. The noise of building quickly fell silent and as quickly resumed. No one was more aware of C. W. Rapp's central role in the firm than George Rapp, who was deeply shaken. His reaction was one thing he shared with his sister-in-law Mary P. R. Rapp. C. W.'s death occurred just at the finish of Washington, D.C.'s National Press Building and Fox Theatre, a 13-story office, club and theatre complex on the southeast corner of 14th Street West and North F Street. The opening gala for this major building attracted everyone in the nation's capitol who mattered, including President and Grace Coolidge. According to Mary it was overwork on this large and detailed project that killed her husband. His funeral was held in the Carbondale Presbyterian Church he designed and helped his father build in 1906. C.W. died little more than a month following the Oriental Theatre opening and just before the industry's transition to talking pictures. The movie palace world he left behind was one of extravagant stage productions and silent films accompanied by room-filling organ music.

For the rest of her life, which lasted another quarter century, Mary always wore clothes in the mourning tones of black or deep purple. Under the terms of Rapp & Rapp's partnership agreement, Mary suddenly shared more than grief with George. She now owned half interest in the firm. She and George recognized that she had no place as an active member of the firm, nor had she any wish for it. Lawyers drew up papers and George bought his sister-in-law's half, making him the sole owner of C. W. & Geo. L. Rapp, Architects, and leaving Mary a very wealthy widow. Mary dealt with her loss by traveling to Europe, taking along her sister's son Franklin. The cultivated Franklin Brewer was always a willing traveling companion who never liked lingering in Chicago. "What has Chicago got," he once remarked, "but the Loop and the lake front? The rest is miles of three-story tenements."

Along with Franklin, Mary traveled with her custom-made Cadillac, which was sent east by train, hoisted aboard ship and stored for the voyage. Because she liked to drive and never had a chauffeur, she ordered the car manufactured with probably the earliest use of wrap-around glass, along with raised seats and extended foot pedals to allow for her short stature. Touring around Europe she was a constant curiosity; a duchess without a driver. In the 1950s the Rapp office was contacted by General Motors asking the auto's whereabouts and offering to buy it back as a museum piece, but the car had gone long before.

The National Press building, club and Fox Theatre, Washington, D. C., clad in silver and gray Atlantic terra cotta, was the job on which C. W. Rapp worked himself to death, according to his widow. (Art. Adams Collection)

In July, the month following his brother's death, George distracted himself by finishing plans for the Mineral Lake lodge. An escapist concept far away from Chicago and New York, the rustic building would occupy a site in the midst of a large north woods tract George bought from the government for pennies an acre, located south of the Bad River Indian Reservation on the edge of what in 1933 would become Chequamegon National Forest. Served by the Soo Line railroad, the town of Mellen was ten miles away from George's place. The nearest city was Ashland, Wisconsin, forty miles distant on the Lake Superior shore. The closest Rapp & Rapp theatre, and one of the earliest, was in Superior, Wisconsin, seventy miles west near Duluth. Closer by in the Hayward, Wisconsin, area was a lodge built at the same time in 1926-27, so similar in design and construction to George Rapp's at Mineral Lake that local lore has long attributed it to Rapp. That lodge was built for a Chicago millionaire named Jacob Loeb, a fellow Standard Club member known by Barney Balaban, who had a Wisconsin summer home of his own. Jacob Loeb was uncle of Richard Loeb, who with Nathan Leopold in the 1920s "crime of the century" murdered young Bobby Franks and set all their names in infamy.

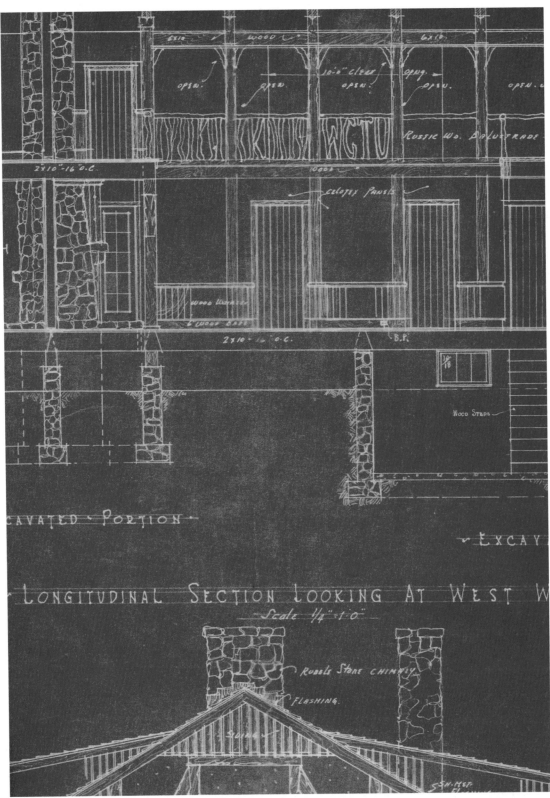

A portion of George Rapp's design from 1926 for his escapist lodge at Mineral Lake near Mellen, Wisconsin. (Rapp Collection)

The Rapp lodge used local materials wherever possible; the foundation and chimney of field and rubble stone, the siding of timbers halved with tongue and groove in a Mellen sawmill. The roof was a double thickness of mule-hide shingles. Joined by separate flues, back-to-back fireplaces shared a chimney, the largest facing the vaulted living room and the other serving an adjoined enclosed sun porch doubling as a dining room. A gasoline-powered Kohler generator installed in an outbuilding provided electricity. When the last light was turned off at night the generator automatically shut down. Cooking was done on a wood-burning stove. Outside was an icehouse, replenished each winter with blocks sawed from the frozen lake and stored through summer in beds of sawdust.

During construction of the lodge, George sent his office man Peter Hoffman up to Mineral Lake to supervise the job and keep away poachers and squatters. His only neighbors were bear and beaver. A caretaker named John Frank replaced Hoffman when the job was finished. He watched over the rustic fiefdom when George wasn't there, which was most of the time. Frank kept the place up and over time built an outlying chicken house and a fenced farmyard where he kept pigs, all very foreign to George, whose cat was his only experience with animals.

Overlooking the lodge living room on three sides was a balcony with a birch-log balustrade. At one end the balusters spelled out the name "Rapp" flanked by "Chi" and "NY". Elsewhere were

Office rendering of Rapp & Rapp's 27-story Old Dearborn (Lake-State) Bank building (1928) at 203 N. Wabash, Chicago. The bank failed in the Depression but the building still stands. (Rapp Collection)

Lake-State bank's upper exterior holds some of Arthur Adams' finest ornament, lost to street-level viewers. (Chicago History Museum)

Lake-State (Old Dearborn) Bank rising in the spirit of Chicago's old Fort Dearborn. (Art Adams Collection)

the Greek letters of George's college fraternity, ΣX. Guests with a sense of humor got the bitter joke behind the birch lettering in the stairway-railing balustrade leading up to the balcony, which spelled WCTU, the anti-liquor Woman's Christian Temperance Union. The lodge became an odd combination of north woods rusticity and haphazard elegance, with oriental rugs, Egyptian hangings, bronze lamps, heavy furniture and roaring fireplaces. Like any Rapp & Rapp theatre, here was another temple to good times.

Business was booming in 1927 when the office published a 90-page hardbound catalog titled The Recent Work of C. W. & Geo. L. Rapp, Architects, with locations shown as Chicago and New York. On the cover was a raised rendering of the Times Square Paramount Building and inside were many pages of photographs selected to show the scope of major work, including theatres, apartment and office buildings and hotels. The back pages featured paid advertisements from contractors, suppliers, boilermakers, electric and lighting companies and others. The ads were congratulatory, expressing pride in having been associated with the buildings of Rapp & Rapp. For the Rapp office, the catalog presented a confident statement about the future following the senior partner's death the previous year.

10 | SOUTHTOWN BLUES

On Chicago's south side in the 1980s, local promoters looked for a place to house their planned New Regal Theatre. The choice was between the Avalon Theatre at 79th and Stony Island, designed by John Eberson in 1927, and Rapp & Rapp's 1931 Southtown at 63rd and Wallace. The Southtown had stopped showing movies in the late 1950s and was used as a discount department store, which closed in 1986. The cost of reconverting the Southtown into the New Regal would have been high. By comparison, except for a white interior paint job, the atmospheric Avalon, then an African-American church, remained intact. Cost comparisons couldn't justify recapturing the Southtown, and in 1991 the last big movie palace built by Rapp & Rapp, and technically perhaps its finest, was reduced to dust.

By 1931, the Rapp office had transformed the art of theatre design into a technique, and with the Spanish-deco-moderne Southtown everything they had learned in the decade following the Chicago and Tivoli came into play. The 3.200 seat theatre's large footprint gave the architects greater space to do better what they had always done best. C. W. Rapp's fixation with sight lines had carried forward into the Southtown, in which an easier slope to the balcony gave patrons the illusion of viewing the stage from the main floor. Stair treads and risers were so well designed that patrons seemed to glide rather than climb or descend from one level to another. The Rapps' customarily elegant chandeliers now featured more modern tubes of neon amidst the crystal glitter, and much of the ornate dome and ceiling plaster work of earlier years had given way to an artful use of stencil. A deco-moderne waterfall and fish pond attracted strolling patrons, and wide concourses flanking the main floor comfortably led them to stairways and exits. Customer comfort had reached its zenith. Though Rapp & Rapp's north side Uptown Theatre of 1925 had more seats and a grand dome ten stories above grade level, Southtown was the largest movie house in floor square footage that the firm ever

Southtown Theatre's flamingo pool and fish pond focal point of the grand lobby. The 1931 Southtown was Rapp & Rapp's last movie palace, fittingly built for longtime clients Balaban & Katz. (Rapp Collection)

Southtown interior with its shallow balcony and no mezzanine boxes. Without box seats , the lower balcony gave patrons the illusion of viewing the stage from the main floor. (Rapp Collection)

built. Fittingly it was done for Balaban & Katz, Rapp & Rapp's most loyal and important clients through the movie palace golden age.

Well into those prosperous years in 1924 Rapp & Rapp built the Windermere East Hotel, opposite the Rosenwald Museum (Museum of Science and Industry), formerly the Palace of Fine Arts for the Columbian Exposition of 1893. The transient and residential hotel became a new home for Mary Gerardi "Grandmary" Rapp of Trinidad, the southern Colorado city where she was born, grew up, married and gave birth to her children. With her son Mason now at the University of Illinois and daughter Mary about to enter the University of Wisconsin, the family's center of gravity was shifting away from Colorado. Importantly, Chicago offered the medical and surgical facilities her younger son William Hamilton needed to fight the effects of polio. She enrolled Bill in the University of Chicago Laboratory School and managed her financial interests from afar, using brothers-in-law Ham and banker Charles Rapp as her Trinidad contacts.

Chicago was now the center of life for Mary and her family. From I. H. and W. M. Rapp's arrival from Carbondale, Illinois, in the late 19th century, Trinidad had been a city of steady progress, but just a few years after Grandmary came to Chicago things began to change. The year 1928 marked the turning point when the southern Colorado coal mines began to close, as the center for the coal industry shifted to southern Illinois. This was an irony for the Rapps, who had left there for Colorado in the first place. Trinidad's steady decline was interrupted only briefly during World War II when steel mills in Pueblo needed Colorado coke for the war effort.

From the University of Chicago lab school, Bill was enrolled in a private school in Lake Forest, Illinois, whose parsimonious administration routinely charged his mother for minor items, like a broken chair or glass which resulted from the boy's attempts to cope with his disability. For high school Bill went to the Todd School in Woodstock, Illinois. Over the following years Grandmary and brother-in-law George met frequently for dinner either on her side of Cornell Avenue at the

Dining room of the Italian liner Conte Grande. The ship carried Grandmary Rapp and her family to Europe in 1929, the summer before Mason Rapp joined his uncles' firm in Chicago. (Rapp Collection)

Conte Grande's writing room. (Rapp Collection)

Windermere East or on his at the Windermere West. It was convenient enough in all weather because of a stylish hallway, lined with soft chairs and drapery that Rapp & Rapp designed to pass under Cornell Avenue and join the two hotels.

It was still something of an unwritten law in 1929, when Mason finished at the University of Illinois, that architects needed a grand tour of Europe as his uncles had done in their turn—Mase's Uncle Ham even took a world tour, while his Uncle Ward (C.W.) had spent six months in Japan (which never seemed to influence his architecture). To that end Bill's mother sold her Southern Pacific Railway shares and packed her three children aboard the Italian liner Conte Grande bound for the Bay of Naples, a ship so ornate that Rapp & Rapp might have designed it. Naples rested below the mountains and the little city of Viggiano from which nearly sixty years earlier Grandmary's father Pasquale Gerardi had immigrated to America. She was not curious about the out-of-the- way Viggiano, and so it was not on the itinerary.

The Conte Grande crossing was quiet and uneventful but for one evening when the Rapps dined at the captain's table. It was the time of Mussolini and, according to Mason's recollection, a woman among the American guests bluntly asked the captain, "If Il Duce asked you to sink this ship with all aboard would you do it?" The captain replied, "Absolutely, Madam." It didn't happen, and Mason was able to appreciate Italy's architecture and sketch his way around Naples, Rome, Venice and Florence. Polio kept his little brother Bill from walking through the Roman Forum, so Mase carried him along piggyback. When someone later asked Bill how he liked Italy he replied, "Fine, except for all the foreigners." Mase's pen and ink drawings from the trip were proficient by any standards, but in later years in a fit of house cleaning he sent them out with the garbage. Called out afterwards on this carelessness he said the drawings were not very good. He was prone to such underestimations, as in 1974 when the Theatre Historical Society of America presented him with its Marquee Award and he wondered why.

After the stock market crash of 1929 Grandmary Rapp was able to buy back at depressed prices the Southern Pacific shares she'd sold to pay for the Italian trip. Ever after she was able to joke that she took her family to Europe on the Southern Pacific. In September 1929, one month before the Wall Street crash ushered-in the Great Depression, Mason fulfilled the destiny others had worked out for him and, with his Uncle Ward only three years dead, went to work in Chicago for Uncle George. In that September the Rapp office flourished, as the Kings and Jersey, their two big "Wonder Theatres" for Marcus Loew, opened to great fanfare on the east coast.

The market crash had no immediate effect on Rapp & Rapp. While Arthur Adams lost heavily in farm loan securities, George Rapp had only a few stocks bought through his broker at Hornblower & Weeks, and he watched with bemusement as they lost value. The office itself was booming as it had for years. Mason's starting salary was $100 a month, generous for someone just out of college. As the jobs came in Mason was expected to pull his weight with no delay. Immediately he went to work on Paramount theatres in Stapleton and Middletown, New York, and another in Lynn, Massachusetts. A month before Mason's arrival, George had applied for a license to practice architecture in California. For too long he had watched plentiful work go to others in that key western state and it seemed time to get involved.

Warner Brothers had come on board with houses in Erie and West Chester, Pennsylvania; Gardner, Massachusetts and a classical French/Art Deco theatre the Warner brothers dedicated as a memorial to their parents and as a tribute to their home town of Youngstown, Ohio. For the exhibiting company Lubliner & Trinz, the Rapps worked-up a complete set of drawings for a full-blown Italianate movie palace called the Gateway at Lawrence Avenue and Lipps in Chicago. In 1930 they worked on a Paramount for Charlottesville, Virginia, designed in the spirit of Jeffersonian classicism (Mason always admired Thomas Jefferson's architecture) and they offered proposals for Paramount theatres in Brussels, Glasgow and Belfast. By the end of 1931 Rapp & Rapp was flattered to be called as consultants on the Radio City Music Hall in New York, the largest and last great entertainment palace of them all. All this and more passed through the Rapp office machinery as if it would never end. Confidence still reigned as George wrote an authoritative chapter titled History of Cinema Theater Architecture for a book called Living Architecture published in 1930 by A. Kroch of Chicago. The late B. A. C. Fowler, a founder of the Theatre Historical Society of America, once remarked that to his tastes the best time in the country was the 22 years between the world wars. The staff at Rapp & Rapp might have agreed with about half of that.

By 1932, after the flush 1920s, the Great Depression finally had its day at Rapp & Rapp. People blamed the stock market crash for the grinding loss of confidence that continued to wear away the economy. The result for Rapp & Rapp, even while their existing theatres were coining money for movie studios and managers, was to fall from a drafting room full of work to just one completed job in 1932; a sweet shop in Winnetka, Illinois, for James Poulos. The office had hit the proverbial brick wall. George had three nephews on his payroll for whom he felt responsible, and a full staff in the drafting room with virtually nothing to do. He put his unoccupied secretary Veronica Walsh to work updating office records and discarding old plans and drawings.

As the fall had happened quickly, so might it end quickly. Such was the hope, and for months George held the status quo. The New York office became a drain, and people began to grumble that if C. W. Rapp were around he would have shut it down immediately. George avoided that move as Ted Bullock kept insisting he had many leads with new work just around the corner. As time went on with nothing coming in and all the costs coming out of George's pocket, it became clear that anything New York might do Chicago could do more cheaply. George belatedly closed the doors on the Paramount Building office and offered to keep Ted on in Chicago. Bullock declined, deciding to stay in New York and work on his own. Bullock's post-Rapp & Rapp work through the 1940s and 50s included the Mars Theatre in Mars, Pennsylvania, 1950; the U. S. Theatre in Hoboken, New Jersey; Syosset Theatre, Syosset, New York; Meadowbrook Theatre, East Meadow, New York and the Port Cinema, Newburyport, Massachusetts.[1]

At the time Bullock left Rapp & Rapp there was carnage at the Chicago office as 130 draftsmen and designers were let go by the numbers. George was advised to hire a press agent to attract business but he was skeptical. Basically he believed that professional work was its own best advertising. He always dismissed even simple brochures as "folded bullshit." Dan Brush had to move from his north shore home in Glencoe to find one nearby that he could afford, while his wife Evelyn earned what she could by giving French lessons. Mason's pay was reduced by half. Other job openings were nearly nonexistent, but Mason heard of one for a designer at Porcelain Enamel Company. George seemed eager to have his nephew off the payroll, but by the time Mason inquired the job was gone. People around the office took up collections to pay apartment utility bills for those who fell behind. The office's right hand man Peter Hoffman left then too, after a dozen years at Rapp & Rapp. Always the optimist, Mason had the idea of putting his meager savings into shares of Samuel Insul's electricity empire, but his wife Virginia, whom he married in 1930, reasoned him out of it—a good thing too since more than a half million shareholders were wiped out when Insul's company collapsed in 1934.

As for George, he was burning through his own money just to keep Rapp & Rapp breathing. Not knowing if the fee would ever be paid, the office began alterations on the Omaha Orpheum (Rapp & Rapp, 1926), which had gone into receivership. At the time Balaban & Katz was building the Southtown they had relieved the troubled Lubliner & Trinz of its Gateway Theatre site and wanted Rapp & Rapp's earlier movie palace scheme for Lubliner scaled back. The office did so in increments, hoping to put over the largest job they could. It was not unusual for the office to prepare sketches for jobs they never got. In fact they drew-up more than 1,100 proposals during the 1920s and 30s, most of which were the dead-end cost of doing business.[2] Isaac Hamilton Rapp once filed suit and lost in Las Vegas, New Mexico, over an unfinished job he'd planned and never got paid for.

Similarly, the Gateway Theatre in Chicago was not a proposal but a full set of finished drawings for a movie palace colossus with full stage and dressing rooms. Under B&K the job became an atmospheric movie theatre with no performing stage or orchestra pit, and with its silver screen flat against the back wall. The rapid series of design changes for the Gateway meant using a lot of office tracing paper quickly, which marked the practical end of the old ink on linen tracings and the cumbersome corrective pasters. Economics always rules architecture and speed serves economy. The idea that architectural drawings needed anything so permanent as linen passed away at Rapp & Rapp with the Great Depression.

1932 was Rapp & Rapp's darkest night and 1933 didn't dawn any brighter. Making matters worse was word from Trinidad in March that George's brother Isaac Hamilton Rapp, the eldest of Isaac Rapp's sons, died at 78 of a heart attack. I. H. Rapp's last job had been the 1931 commanding officer's home at Roswell's New Mexico Military Institute, built in harmony with the Collegiate Gothic style of the rest of the campus developed by I. H. & W. M. Rapp beginning in 1908. In June, 1930, with former partners Will Rapp and Arthur Hendrickson ten years dead, I. H. Rapp acknowledged his own mortality by promoting his office superintendent, giving the firm its final name: I. H. & W. M. Rapp and Francis W. Spencer, Architects. After I. H. died, Spencer worked on his own designing a Pueblo Revival ranch house for Trinidad's Joe Tarabino, completed in 1934. Hamilton Rapp's death left George the last of his brother architects, just as the ravages of the 1930s were having their way.

The 2008 failure of the credit and securities markets justifiably stirred fear and concern, but even with that, present generations might not understand fully the heavy financial and psychological toll exacted by the Great Depression. To those who lived through its worst, the effects were life changing. The excess and optimism of the 1920s devolved quickly into an entrenched loss of confidence. Without deposit insurance 4,000 banks across the country fell to bank runs while other business failures accumulated. Unemployment at its worst claimed at least 25% of the working-age population, and the stock market between 1929 and 1932 lost 90 percent of its value. People stopped spending and saved what money they had, which only meant more job loss. During the long Depression many Americans lost faith in business and even capitalism in general, some drifting toward seductive socialist and communist ideas. Those who weren't so tempted nevertheless were left with a lifelong suspicion of debt and waste. Children were taught to take care of their belongings to make them last. Caution, frugality and prudence became chief virtues. Traumatized by the Depression, Mason never thought in terms of any "good old days," and because of Rapp & Rapp's sudden fall the office stayed small for the rest of its days.

In the depths of this unrelieved gloom, deliverance suddenly arrived in the person of one C. C. "Cash & Carry" Pyle. Pyle was a versatile professional promoter famous at the time for his "Bunion Derby," a 1928 Oklahoma foot race organized to publicize the cross country highway Route 66. He had also a financial interest in the Champaign Orpheum when Rapp & Rapp built it in 1914. In 1925 he became the world's first sports agent by representing University of Illinois football star Harold "Red" Grange when he signed with the Chicago Bears. Now C. C. Pyle was stalking a new opportunity, the 1933 Chicago World's Fair called the Century of Progress Exposition, scheduled to open in the summer. Pyle wanted a museum/arcade to display Robert Ripley's strange and grotesque collections from around the world. The building was to be called "Ripley's Believe it or Not Odditorium," and its architecture was to be appropriately exotic. The catch was that Pyle

Office rendering of Rapp & Rapp's Oriental Village for the "Century of Progress" Chicago World's Fair of 1933. This project saved Rapp & Rapp from extinction in the depths of the Great Depression. (Rapp Collection)

had no money up front, so the desperate George Rapp gambled on a percentage of the gate. The Odditorium became first among the most popular exhibits at the fair, along with another Rapp building called the Oriental Village. With these successes the office, while not free of problems, avoided immediate extinction.

The 1933 fair was a buoyant public reminder of how America ought to be, meeting such success that it was held over into 1934, the most miserably hot summer of the Dust Bowl years. Rapp & Rapp came back with fresh alterations to the Odditorium. Energized by victory, the firm grasped for more fair work by drawing-up proposals for a Press Building and Publishers' Club and a Hearst Newspaper and Magazine Building, neither of which was built. Other imaginative failures were Mason's proposal for Proctor & Gamble, a giant bar of Ivory Soap floating in a reflecting pool and an idea ahead of its time called the Micky Mouse Theatre. The office had crawled out of its hole and morale was on the upswing; but things were different. C. W. & Geo. L. Rapp, Architects, was a lot smaller and a lot less mighty than it had been a few years before. The core staff remained; George Rapp, Dan Brush, Charles McCarthy, Arthur Adams and Mason; but with few others, the hallways echoed.

The rejuvenating effect of the Chicago fair inspired others, and in 1935 San Diego opened the California Pacific International Exposition on the Balboa Park site used for the Panama California Exposition in 1915. I. H. & W. M. Rapp's Pueblo Revival style State of New Mexico Building was slated for an auditorium enlargement, to become the Palace of Education for the 1935 fair. With the Trinidad Rapps gone, George and the Chicago office were hired to design the job.

After repeal of Prohibition in 1933, the idea of designing large night clubs infused with Rapp & Rapp style seemed a bright one. The firm after all had catered to public taste in this way before when in 1921 they built the popular Trianon ballroom for Andrew Karzas on the south side of Chicago.

A complete aerial view of the Oriental Village rendered by the office in 1933. (Art. Adams, Jr. Collection)

It was still not clear to Rapp & Rapp that palatial grandeur was working its way out of style, and because elegant night clubs lacked the profit-making mass appeal of movies the idea came to nothing. For the moment, the office had to be satisfied with various renovations and improvements for the Windermere East Hotel, including Grandmary Rapp's own apartment.

The Rapp office never left theatre work and theatre work never left them, but one thing became clear by 1935: movie houses were getting smaller. For Balaban & Katz, the Rapps altered the Chicago Theatre marquee, added improvements to the smaller Apollo Theatre on Randolph Street and built a modern movie house flanked by one story commercial spaces on Chicago's west side at Belmont and Parkside. The theatre was called Will Rogers, for the man from Oklahoma whose wit lifted American spirits during the Depression. For opening day, rose petals were flown in from New York and dropped over the Will Rogers site. All along, the office was called in by various theatre managements

Cartoon by Carey Orr in the Chicago Tribune hit home for Mason Rapp in 1932. He kept it framed on his office wall. (Rapp Collection)

for simple fire code upgrades or adjustments to the ever newer and larger theatre lobby concession counters. Sometimes small alterations, which might take no more than an afternoon, got in the way of larger jobs, but the office always remembered hard times and never turned down any work.

Concession counters were latecomers to theatre design. Strict fire codes legislated after the Iroquois Theater fire in 1903 meant that cooking inside theaters was prohibited, though nothing prevented restaurant entrepreneurs from operating next door. Many early theatres had these neighboring establishments, and movie house managers could only covet the profits. One Chicago enterprise named C. Cretors & Company changed all this, and in the process grew rich while other businesses sank. Charles Cretors had invented the street vending popcorn machine in 1885. As the movie industry developed, his company found a way to beat the fire codes while still conforming to them by bringing fresh popcorn into theatres and keeping it heated. Theatre profits from popcorn sales rose accordingly and managers quickly introduced candy, chewing gum and soft drinks. Ultimately theatres made more money from concessions than they did from ticket sales. Rapp & Rapp concession counter upgrades continued through the 1950s.

In the late 1930s Barney Balaban's brothers Harry and Elmer planned to develop a site for a new theatre on Oak Street in Chicago's Gold Coast, and Mason went after the job. Despite his efforts, the Esquire Theatre went to architects Pereira & Pereira, and it was one of only two occasions when Mase groused about a job he thought he should have had but didn't get (the other was the late-1950s Sigma Chi national headquarters in Evanston, Illinois, which he said went to another because of "politics").

Hard times took a visible toll on George Rapp. He became more passive around the office and expected Mason to represent Rapp & Rapp at meetings and social functions. After one party put on by theatre management, a scandalized young Mason reported back to his uncle that there were girls there who on cue leapt hardly dressed from large cakes, and danced on tables. His world-weary uncle was not impressed and only replied, "Tarts, eh?" Still nominally in charge of the office, George handed off ever more responsibility to Mason, at one point instructing his nephew about the pitfalls of an overly eager design department whose flights of fancy could be costly. "Watch the design boys," said George.

With the faint scent of economic recovery in the air in 1936, Rapp & Rapp sought to win back the Warner Brothers work that had fallen away with the Depression after the office designed the elegant 2500 seat art deco Warner Theatre (1931) in Milwaukee. The man to see toward this end was Warner's chief of construction Herman Maier, whom the office conspired to wine and dine at the Chez Paree, Chicago's celebrated night club. On hand were Adams, Brush, McCarthy and Mason. George Rapp financed the outing but didn't attend. The dinner meeting was a high time with lots of laughs and free-flowing alcohol. Things got clownish and spun out of hand when Dan Brush grabbed a seltzer bottle from the table and, mimicking the movie cliché, accidentally sprayed Maier in the face. In effect he had sprayed Warner Brothers in the face. Maier was embarrassed and outraged while the rest, especially Brush, were in shock. Mase rushed around the table and escorted Maier to the door. With repeated apologies he walked Maier around the block and over to a Michigan Avenue shop where he bought him a new tie. The party was over and Mason thought Warner Brothers lost forever; but Maier proved forgiving. From this social fiasco came Warner's Rhodes Theatre at 79th and Rhodes on Chicago's south side that opened in 1937 and proved a watershed in many ways for

Rapp & Rapp. Two theatres planned in 1937 that didn't go through would have been done for Sam C. Myers, a north shore theatre owner related by marriage to the Balabans. These were the Glenwin, on the border between Glencoe and Winnetka, and the Bay Theatre planned for Wilmette. Together their cost would have amounted to half a million dollars.

Even without the Glenwin and Bay, all the activity and interest coupled with the successful Rhodes job convinced Mason that the hard times might be starting to lift. The pace of work that followed tended to confirm this judgment. Among these jobs were more of Rapp & Rapp's continual updates to their earlier theatres, including front and lobby treatments for Arthur Schoenstadt's Peoples Theatre, and basement alterations for the Chicago. For the Great States Theatre Company the firm reworked the front and lobby of the Palace in Peoria. Through McCarthy, the office got the job of designing

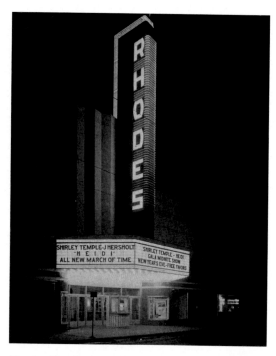

Rhodes Theatre marquee and vertical sign.
(Chicago History Museum)

and installing the skating rink at the Chicago Arena on McClurg Court, formerly the Chicago Riding Academy and later headquarters for CBS radio and television. Mac had been an Olympic ice skater and knew people in figure skating, including Michael Kirby and Sonja Hennie. The office even added a new marquee to their 1915 example of elegance for all movie palaces everywhere, the Al. Ringling in Baraboo, Wisconsin.

Both small and large, the jobs were picking up and the pace accelerating, but the happy arrival of the Rhodes Theatre had a darker side: the days of grand design and ornament, both classical and fanciful, were over. With the neighborhood Rhodes it was clear that less had become more. Movies had established themselves and no longer needed the backup of a full vaudeville stage; and now that films had sound there was less need for accompanying high-powered Wurlitzer pipe organs and the towering decorative organ grilles that flanked the proscenium arches. The Rhodes was drawn up on tracing paper in what, by comparison to the old work, seemed perfunctorily modern lines. In short, the original palatial concepts of C.W. and George Rapp had gone away and the Beaux-Arts design magic of Arthur Frederick Adams became vestigial.

Adams knew the situation, and when in 1937 George Rapp let him go he understood. George's faithful and efficient secretary Veronica Walsh left then too. Unlike Adams she was ready to retire to her large apartment in a baronial building on the lake in the north shore suburb of Evanston. Adams himself had designed his own French Provincial home in 1934 in Wilmette, one fashionable suburb north of Evanston, and he continued to work in Chicago. He helped design Midway Airport, built the Fountain Square Building in Evanston, and in the 1950s worked for Naess & Murphy on the

After a long absence Warner Brothers came back to Rapp & Rapp in 1937 for Chicago's south side Rhodes Theatre. This suggested to Mason Rapp that the Great Depression's hard times for the office might be lifting. (Chicago History Museum)

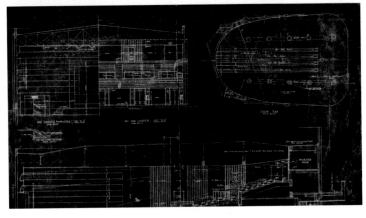

Plan, elevation and section of the Rhodes, drawn in 1936, reveal a spare design approach for Rapp & Rapp. Times had changed away from ornate, and expensive, movie palaces in the decade following C. W. Rapp's death. (Chicago History Museum)

Prudential Building, Chicago's first high-rise structure since the Depression. But never again did he use all his skills as variously as he had at Rapp & Rapp.

Other neighborhood theatres followed along; the Ciné and in 1939 the little Luna at 4743 W. Belmont featuring moderne aeronautical motifs and state-of-the-art seating. The Luna, the 47th theatre in the Balaban & Katz chain, was "as streamlined as a skyliner," according to Mason as reported in the Chicago Evening American. The news story went on to point out Rapp & Rapp's use of teardrop-shaped lighting fixtures resembling airplane wings, tubular exterior lighting and "a streamlined neon filled with uranium high-powered gas which defies fog." The Depression seemed to be loosening its grip on Rapp & Rapp but would only let go completely after the ordeal of the war that lay just ahead.

In 1939 the office replaced the 28-year-old Lexington Theatre, 1162 E. 63rd Street, with a flashy new venue called the Lex. The marquee was built of porcelain with fittings of stainless steel, while the facade featured fluted glass brick and high-powered neon. Inside, Rapp & Rapp lowered the volume by using soft fluorescent lighting, a new technology. As one newspaper put it, regarding new theatres of this sort, "Theatre design has gone a long way in discarding old architectural forms. In the new streamline design, mass, color and line have replaced a profusion of ornament which was the accepted practice a few years back." A theatre became, like a sculpture, its own ornament.

11 | THE FORTIES

By the end of the 1930s a move for the office was overdue. For years the State-Lake spaces they moved into in 1918 had been too big for Rapp & Rapp. Now, furriers began to occupy the lower floors and clients were noticing the smell of mothballs. Inertia was overcome in 1940 when George left the past behind by moving the operation two blocks east into the 40-story green, gold and black art deco Carbide & Carbon building, 230 N. Michigan Avenue. The Carbide building was designed a decade before for Union Carbide by Burnham Brothers, Daniel and Hubert, the sons of the Daniel Burnham who headed design and construction for the Chicago Columbian Exposition of 1893, designed Marshall Field's, built Orchestra Hall and laid out the grand plan to preserve Chicago's lake front as an open park.

Rapp & Rapp moved into the fourth floor at the northeast corner overlooking Michigan Avenue and South Water Street. George took the corner office adjoining the drafting room where McCarthy worked, while Dan Brush and Mason moved into two offices to the west with northern exposures overlooking Water Street. Here Rapp & Rapp remained for the rest of its days. Shortly after the move, George officially turned the office over to Mason, Brush and McCarthy as equal partners, withdrawing himself from the mix. He said to Mase, "Do what you can with it."

Even though business was good and getting better, George long had appeared lethargic and uninterested. Out of a sense of obligation through the bitter 1930s he had spent most of his money keeping the office afloat. His family had a history of mutual obligation. His brothers and father Isaac had paid to put him through architecture school, and in the days before corporate and government safety nets all the boys had rallied around to help support Isaac and mother Georgeina in their old age. George Rapp in his turn had his nephews to watch out for, not to mention the memory and example

Among the furnishings moved in the 1940s from the State-Lake Building to Rapp & Rapp's Carbide Building quarters at 230 N. Michigan was this gothic cabinet from George Rapp's office. (Rapp Collection)

Ulster chairs surrounded the main conference table of the same style in George Rapp's original State-Lake office. They survived the move to the Carbide Building, though much else was left behind. (Rapp Collection)

of his brothers in Trinidad and his former senior partner in Chicago. It was a serious legacy, and to that extent he had no choice. Rather than abandon the office he trusted to time and procrastination.

Now without enough money to afford both his Windermere West apartment and the lodge at Mineral Lake, George had another decision ahead. A hallway adapted from abutting closet spaces connected the double apartment. With this alteration George had created space he never really needed. Aside from a few years in which his cash-strapped nephew Ted Bullock took a room, George lived alone there for more than thirty years. He enjoyed hosting small groups of friends and family. Guests usually were in for a long cocktail hour and 10 p.m. dinner, not that they objected. It was the urban style of the times. Gathering point for small parties was a seating area around the fireplace. George liked to sit in an armchair positioned a little behind the main group, a participant but a bit removed. House man Robert circulated to keep the drinks fresh. Eventually George with a nod would signal Robert to serve dinner; most often steak, baked potato and asparagus. Robert was no gourmet chef, but a good short order cook.

The apartment was filled with a motley but oddly harmonious collection of stuff accumulated through the years: batik-draped bronze lamps; cloisonné vases; odd sconces, bowls and ash trays; battered silver-plated Windermere serving dishes; couches and chairs arranged in seating areas—and oriental room rugs, prayer rugs and runners. The orientals were good, but few were free of tears, repairs, moth holes from summers without air-conditioning and dullness from the coal soot of city winters. Some rugs were pocked with acid burns from the leaky power supplies of the radio sets George listened to. While some of his furnishings had money value, much else was trivial and utilitarian, all giving the impression of a man who haphazardly came across stuff and was not a serious collector. Nevertheless the place appeared warm and inviting and, thanks to Robert and Adelaide, it was kept up.

These various period pieces and his many wall and ceiling hangings gave the large dim double apartment an exotic appearance, unlike the untheatrical public face of his old 190 N. State Street office. Any clients who expected movie palace decor when they walked into George's office were soon disabused. Though the Rapps were famous for theatre design they always hoped to avoid the potential limitations of a specialist reputation. What office visitors found was a large room decorated in subdued contemporary 1920s style. Antiques weren't excluded, but paneled walls, warm furniture and soft cove lighting at the ceiling set a conservative tone. There were shelves of architectural reference books and technical publications, and at one end a conference table surrounded by carved Ulster chairs. Adjacent was a large built-in lighted display board for presenting plans and renderings, which when not in use was covered by a drawn drapery.

The new offices at 230 N. Michigan were minimalist by comparison. Some nice furniture and books were moved over from the State-Lake for George's office (much of it stored in the Carbide building's basement locker) but the drafting room was a spare workshop with tables, stools and tools. Calendars from contractors and suppliers provided the only wall decoration. As it filled with stacks of trade journals and other publications, the place began to look more established. George was in and out of the office during the transition, but finally decided to close down at the Windermere West and move permanently to Mineral Lake. This meant getting rid of things. Whatever he didn't ship north to the lake he distributed as they wanted between Dan and Mase and to Robert and Adelaide.

Ted Bullock in New York could have claimed some things but declined. With the original Mineral Lake caretaker John Frank suddenly gone amid talk of "a woman," Robert and Adelaide traveled north with George to open the place up and get him settled, with an open offer to stay on. George was something of a mysterious legend around Mellen, Wisconsin, the town nearest to Mineral Lake. To the locals he was the rich and famous big city architect whom few ever saw. At the same time they grumbled that he avoided local merchants and shipped in his food on the Soo Line from Stop & Shop in Chicago.

In time the arrangement came to seem less realistic to Robert and Adelaide. The lodge was isolated, and they were city people with friends and a life back home. George understood, and they agreed to stay on until he could find local replacements. Help arrived from a couple named Charlie and Emma Hawkinson. Charlie had worked for a cheese factory in Mellen. Running a lodge for the famous architect on Mineral Lake offered responsibility and status.

It was no secret to anyone who knew him that George was slipping. He was bloated and puffy from an enlarged heart that left him breathless when he climbed the stairs to his room off the second floor balcony. He began to spend more time in his bedroom, even taking meals there. Meantime Charlie and Emma took hold, kept the place running, and attended the chickens, pigs and a feisty little dog called Nig. Dan Brush periodically visited with his wife and two children, who frolicked off the dock in the copper-tinted Mineral Lake. Mason went at other times with his wife and sister. Even C. W. Rapp's widow (the Brush family referred to her as Aunt Mary Ward to distinguish her from Mase's mother who to them was Aunt Mary Will and to close family members was Grandmary) seemed to soften her silent disapproval of George. She knew that her inherited share of Rapp & Rapp weathered the Depression in blue chip bonds while George's capital withered subsidizing the struggling office. In a small but significant gesture she shipped to George two bottles of scotch whisky packed in excelsior, but by then it was too late to apologize. George, after insisting on his right to drink all through Prohibition, had cut out alcohol months before and replaced it with iced tea.

As the office in Chicago continued without him, George's quiet life at Mineral Lake went on into 1941. At last unable to manage the stairs, he spent his last few months in his bedroom. Emma cooked and Charlie brought up the meals, until one morning it was over. The end for George was solitary and ignominious. Charlie found him in the bathtub where he had fallen. His death at age 63 was attributed to cerebral hemorrhage and congestive heart failure. With no special memorial service, Mason and Brush had their uncle's cremated remains shipped to Carbondale and interred in his mother's grave. George may have wanted no more than this. He was not outwardly religious, and claimed he was an atheist. Other times he said he had his own religion. Some people have wondered whether he was related to the George Rapp of New Harmony, Indiana, who founded the 19th century celibate "Rappite" religious commune. This was not true.

In his will George left everything in equal parts to his three nephews. The bequest included the Mineral Lake lodge, its contents, and little else. With Charlie and Emma Hawkinson still on hand the lodge became a summer vacation destination at different times for the Brush and Rapp families. C. W.'s widow Mary, who had never seen George's lodge, went along with the Rapps. Always wearing her dark mourning dresses, she liked the relaxation of fishing from the rowboat but refused to bait the hook or touch the fish she caught. She also took to gathering eggs from the hen house, shooing the chickens off their nests with her full skirts. To pass the time Mason began taking the rowboat out alone, experimenting for hours with the principles of sailing. The green lap strake boat was not built for the purpose, but Mase stepped a makeshift mast and, using a bed sheet for a mainsail and a gunny sack for a jib, tried to make it function. Rigging clothesline for main and jib sheets, he worked to find the breeze, but without a centerboard the boat only moved sideways whenever the rag sails filled. Success was elusive but he was learning.

George lived just long enough to hear that his brother Ham's widow Jean died of a sudden heart attack in May 1941. Following Ham's death eight years earlier, she had designed her own Pueblo Revival house in Santa Fe, furnished and decorated with a southwestern feel according to her informed tastes. As widow of the architect whose firm had built so much of value in New Mexico, she became a well-known hostess and patron of the arts. Death came quietly as she sat in a chair at the window overlooking her garden.

The Chicago office continued steadily on without George Rapp. Both in spirit and in fact he had been absent from business for so long that his death had little practical effect. One problem was the residual name of the firm; C. W. & Geo. L. Rapp. People who phoned the office asking for either man had to be told that both were deceased. Mason paid a courtesy call to Mary P. R. Rapp to ask what she thought about a name change for the office that bore her late husband's initials. With her understanding and support, C. W. and Geo. L. were written out of the firm, which in 1942 became simply Rapp & Rapp, Architects. The firm always had been spoken of as Rapp & Rapp but now it was official.

To grab more north light for McCarthy's drafting room, George's corner office was torn out. Mason and Dan Brush kept the same offices but Mase replaced his few furnishings with George's heavy desk, books and the remaining Ulster chairs and conference table brought over from the State-Lake. It was the time of the Swainwood residential development, the wartime Toledo Valentine Theatre renovation and steel extraction, and Ross Auditorium at Great Lakes Naval Training Center.

At the same time, the motion picture studio system was breaking down. Under this system, studios produced their own films with a contracted stable of actors for exclusive exhibition in their own theatres. In 1938, a year after Rapp & Rapp had gotten back with Warner Brothers on the Rhodes Theatre, the Supreme Court ruled the studio system monopolistic. The government filed an antitrust case called United States vs. Paramount Pictures. Suddenly any resurgence the Rhodes seemed to promise was about to be taken away by the courts. Paramount eased some of its booking policies, hoping to lift the legal siege, but the gestures were not enough. Soon it was not just Paramount under assault but the other majors as well, including Warner's, Loew's (MGM), 20th Century Fox and RKO, all for whom Rapp & Rapp had created grand palaces. By 1948 the studios were forced to break the ties that connected production and exhibition. Ironically the studio system likely would have crumbled anyway under competition from television, a business the far-seeing Balaban & Katz had already been exploring. B&K were never sentimental about their magnificent theatres, which closed or were sold whenever they stopped making money. By 1948 it was clear to even the most faithful holdouts that nothing like the grand palaces would ever be built again. As the old houses were getting dirty and worn under years of service, and the early glories were taken for granted by the general public, movie theatre managers had to scramble to justify themselves. Rapp & Rapp had to adjust as well.

As the studio system was crumbling in the Federal courts, Chicago in 1946 experienced its most disastrous fire since the Iroquois Theatre. The old and elegant LaSalle Hotel at La Salle and Madison was designed by Holabird & Roche in 1909 in a Louis Quatorze style-of-the-time, which architects Marshall & Fox used a year later in the elegant Blackstone Hotel on Michigan Avenue. La Salle's lobby and mezzanine carried a lot of old wood and fabric, tinder for the roaring blaze that used the five elevator shafts as chimneys. Fire consumed the lower seven floors, filling the entire building with toxic smoke. Sixty-one people died, most of smoke inhalation.

Avery Brundage, a civil engineer who had been a Dan Brush classmate at the University of Illinois, owned the LaSalle. He became wealthy as a builder and real estate investor, but was best known then and is remembered today for his lifelong connection with amateur athletics, especially the Pan-American Games and the Olympics. A decathlon Olympian himself in the 1912 Stockholm games, Brundage ultimately became president of the International Olympic Committee, idealistically defending against the encroachments of professionalism and politics into what he felt should remain the amateur and non-partisan status of the games. Brundage is also remembered for his vast collection of Asian art, priceless pieces of which were almost carelessly spread around his office like so many knick-knacks. When he decided to donate the full collection, he contacted the Art Institute of Chicago, which, perhaps unaware of what Brundage had, apparently never got back to him. Finally he donated the entirety to San Francisco, where it resides as the Avery Brundage Collection of Asiatic Art.

Following the La Salle disaster, Brush called Brundage to offer sympathies, saying to call if there was anything he could do. Brundage had been general contractor in 1937 on Rapp & Rapp's conversion

Bismarck Hotel, Metropolitan Office Building and Palace Theatre, all combined by Rapp & Rapp into a multi-use Chicago complex in the 1920s. Big jobs like this gave the office the background needed for a 1940s renovation and replacement project following the disastrous La Salle Hotel fire. (Art. Adams, Jr. Collection)

Mason G. Rapp at the time of the La Salle Hotel project. (Rapp Collection)

Ad for the 1920s Leland, Detroit, another Rapp hotel job preceding the 1948 La Salle renovation in Chicago. (Art. Adams, Jr. Collection)

of the Chicago Riding Club into the Chicago Arena, and he knew that in the 1920s Rapp & Rapp had built Detroit's Leland Hotel, and Karl and Otto Eitel's Bismarck Hotel, Palace Theatre and Metropolitan Office Building just up Chicago's La Salle Street at Randolph. With the Bismarck, guests could step from the restful and intimate art deco lobby into a taste of Germany at Old Heidelberg Restaurant, or into the glories of Versailles at the Palace. The new hotel for Brundage would need similar applications. Based on all this background, Brundage hired Rapp & Rapp to rebuild and renovate the La Salle.

The job for Brundage's La Salle-Madison Corporation was called the La Salle Hotel Rehabilitation & Replacement Plan and in 1946 was still subject to the same War Production Board restrictions on strategic materials that had regulated the Valentine Theatre job a few years earlier. The result was far from a restoration of the old royalty in the Holabird & Roche original. Since 1909 when the La Salle was built, America had gone through many shifts in architectural tastes through two world wars and an economic depression. Now times and tastes had changed once more. Rapp & Rapp's answer was a subdued contemporary design with lots of warm wood and bronze ornament, but by comparison to the old La Salle interior it was, in the modern sense, spare. The job was extensive, involving restaurants, cocktail lounges, barber and beauty shops and significant alterations to every level from the basement to the top floor. Many important changes were unseen by hotel guests, including updated ventilation and sprinkler systems throughout. For the 22nd floor paint store-room and match-storage vault sprinkler system, Rapp & Rapp hired consulting engineer John Dolio, who the following year became a partner in the Chicago architectural firm of Shaw, Metz & Dolio.

Of all that was done to put the hotel up to code and back into use, Mason chose to show a visitor the overhead "egg-crate" lighting in the building's corner Walgreen's drug store. This wall-to-wall translucent plastic cross-hatching covered banks of fluorescent tubing, providing a bright, shadowless light that made a good show of the merchandise. It was modern technology and, like his father before him, Mase liked new things.

The pace of work on the La Salle job pressed for the cautious hiring of more help. Through the war years Mason, Dan and Mac had done the architecture, answered phones and spread the paperwork load. Now the search went out via a modest classified ad in the Chicago Tribune that read: SECRETARY—capable stenographer, operate small switchboard, keep simple set of books. Excellent salary for right person. This routine ad caught the attention of Clara Weirauch, who came to provide the greatest operational improvement to the office since George Rapp hired Veronica Walsh.

Clara was from Lewistown, Illinois, in the downstate Spoon River country. (Edgar Lee Masters included a "Weirauch" in his Spoon River Anthology.) Clara left Lewistown for Brown's Business College in Peoria, followed by three semesters in accounting at Northwestern University. After various secretary, stenographer and Comptometer jobs she advanced to run the Payroll and Tax Department at John R. Thompson Company in Chicago, and went on to became secretary to the Illinois Director of Conservation. Bored with a subsequent legal stenographer's job, she answered Rapp & Rapp's ad. When she came for her interview only Brush was there. Without waiting to consult Mason and Mac, he hired Clara at the requested $60 per week.

Within days Brush's snap judgment was vindicated. Files were cleaned out and ordered, stacks of outdated publications were thrown out, bills were paid, phone records were deciphered and categorized, and the glass that separated her receptionist's office from the waiting room vestibule received its first cleaning in many months. She mastered contracts and specifications, took charge of payrolls and taxes, which fluctuated with the pace of work and personnel turnover, and stayed level-headed in all circumstances. Not least among her virtues was her telephone voice and manner; strong, welcoming and intelligent. From then in 1948 to the office's closing (but for one period in the late 1950s when she went back to Lewistown to help with the family business, leaving the Rapp office to a chaotic parade of office temps), Clara's engaging "Good morning, Rapp & Rapp" was the office's public voice.

At nearly the same time, during the La Salle job, Rapp & Rapp took on a University of Illinois design graduate named Edwin Storako. Like Mason's brother Bill, Storako had polio as a boy, consigning him to a life on crutches. In those days this might have hurt employment chances elsewhere, but with Mason it made no difference. Storako's portfolio clearly showed his talent, and he shared with many other polio survivors of his generation a determined, stubborn defiance against his disability.

Edwin B. Storako joined Rapp & Rapp in 1948. A University of Illinois design graduate hired to help on the demanding La Salle job, Storako stayed on to the closing of the office in 1965. (Rapp Collection)

Determination drove Storako even through the smallest details of his life and work, and with it he proved capable and creative, able as Mason said, "to turn out the work of ten men." His versatility was what Rapp & Rapp needed during the following years, when the office moved with the needs of the times, producing drive-up banks, bakeries, car washes, hotels, industrial plants, air line ticket offices, private clubs and as always the theatres, culminating in the early 1960s with the Fisher Theatre renovation in Detroit, a challenging job and Rapp & Rapp's biggest theatre project since Chicago's Southtown in 1931.

12 | SAILING

ncle George's Mineral Lake lodge didn't last long in the hands of his heirs. Unoccupied in the months after George's death, the place became infested with bats hanging from the rafters and draperies. Attempts to snare them with nets or swing at them with farm tools were thwarted by the animals' natural radar. Any bat hanging within reach would drop into a net if tapped with a screwdriver handle, but this method was haphazard and futile. Mason finally called in a contact named Norm Dold who ran a Chicago exterminating business. Dold arrived and lighted oil-burning smudge pots inside the lodge, with instructions to keep out, and let the pots burn through the winter. By spring the bats had gone, but this didn't solve other problems. George may have preferred splendid isolation but his nephews did not.

After a few summers of alternating two-week Brush and Rapp family vacations, and some winter weekends of snowshoes, skis and roaring blazes in the rubble-stone fireplace, the place showed its limitations. Ted Bullock never came in from New York to use the lodge, and retaining the caretakers Charlie and Emma Hawkinson was expensive. Keeping the place also meant having to use it, which removed other family vacation options. The heirs agreed to sell the lodge and property, including George's furnishings, to a group wanting it for a fishing retreat. Years later in the 1980s, the owners sold it all back to the U. S. Government for many times the pennies per acre George Rapp had paid for it. Preservationists had the lodge moved and recycled as a local art center.

Mason's primitive efforts with sailing on Mineral Lake kindled a need to know more. Back in Chicago, after Rapp & Rapp had built Ross Auditorium at Great Lakes, Mase bought a half share in the 22-square-meter class sloop Isis (US 100). A Great Lakes naval officer named Harrison Bordner owned the other half. As a Navy man, Bordner at least knew nautical nomenclature while Mason,

Chicago Yacht Club's Monroe Street Station, designed by Rapp & Rapp in the 1950s. (Chicago History Museum)

Yacht Club interior looking south from the main hallway. (Chicago History Museum)

who grew up in Colorado and New Mexico's high desert, knew little more than port from starboard. This was to change as Isis joined into a small racing fleet of 22-square- meters at Montrose Harbor's Chicago Corinthian Yacht Club. When more boat owners were attracted into this lively group, the fleet changed its venue to larger facilities at Chicago Yacht Club's Belmont Harbor Station, whose unique club-house was built on a floating barge moored to shore. When the Navy transferred Bordner, Mason was joined aboard Isis (by then renamed Foo) by a cigar-smoking partner with a German accent named John Panhausen. Panhausen's business was design and manufacture of injection-molded plastic toys, common today in any shopping mall but new and fascinating technology in the early post-war years.

The graceful and responsive 22s were right for intense sailors. Long, narrow and sleek, these high-masted mahogany boats had one basic design requirement—22 square meters of sail area. This meant individual hull designs varied in size and weight. No two were alike. Ranging

Isis in June, 1946, navigating out of the river toward the Chicago Light and the open waters of Lake Michigan. Isis was first of four 22-square-meters Mason Rapp raced in club competition. (Rapp Collection)

from 35 to 42 feet in length with a maximum six foot beam and five foot draft, the boats could weigh up to 5,000 pounds, with the lead keel accounting for half of that. Since smaller boats had certain weather advantages over the larger, and vice-versa, the boats raced equally without handicaps. In racing, the boats needed a crew of two in addition to the skipper at the tiller; one in the cockpit handling the jib sheets and running back-stays, the other forward to keep the jib clear of fouling on a come-about or jibe; and to rig, hoist and retrieve the spinnaker. A good crew worked with precision.

Below decks the boats were spare. Two narrow bunks separated by a small wooden locker comprised the accommodations. Before the mast was an area, accessible to the deck through a forward hatch, used for sail storage. The crew member assigned to handle the spinnaker used this area as his base of operation. The 22s had no auxiliary engines. They were built for speed under sail.

The 1940s and 50s were the tail end of the centuries-old dominion of wooden boats, with their evocative smells of varnish and oakum caulk. At Belmont Harbor were the big yawls and schooners bearing exotic names—Bangalore, Rubiyat, Polaris, and the majestic Manitou that swung alone on her mooring, heaving on the swells just inside the harbor mouth. Other racing class boats besides the 22s shared the harbor—the 110s, Luders, R boats, Q boats and 10 meters —but among them the 22 sailors seemed the most committed and energetic.

The 22s at Belmont were built in the 1930s and 40s, mostly in Sweden but for a few in Germany and the U. S., by designers like Nilsson, H. Becker, Tör Holm and Knud Reimers. The 22s were derivations of the Scandinavian skerry cutters, from the Swedish word "skär" for the small rock islands of the Baltic shoreline. Tall raked masts curved at the top allowed the mainsail to catch light air between the skerries, and the short booms combined with the top-mast curve gave the mainsails, as one early designer claimed, the shape of a gull's wing. The sails may have looked like wings but they behaved like airfoils. Every boat's uniqueness gave racing sailors room for creative experimentation with canvas, rigging, fittings and even a lot of boat buying and selling to gain the competitive edge. Beyond the short-lived Isis (Foo), Mason in his quest for the grail of victory in club course racing rotated through three more boats named Foo II, Foo III and Defensor.

Foo III arriving in Chicago from Sweden aboard the freighter Helga Smith. (Rapp Collection)

The most successful of these was Foo III (S-208). Built in the 1940s at Rodesund's Batvarv in Gothenburg, S-208 on Mason's order was lashed under canvas aboard the deck of the Swedish freighter Helga Smith and shipped via the St. Lawrence Seaway to Chicago. Mase bought it sight unseen but for design drawings and snapshots of the boat performing among the skerries. With S-208 Mase, into the mid-1950s, perfected the advantage of then new Mylar and Dacron sails, leaving the final winners' dinners with an embarrassment of trophies. The last boat, Defensor (S-222), was a kind of afterthought, so neglected it was practically a salvage job that Mason rescued for $1,500 from a windswept Michigan beach. After investment of time and lots more money Defensor became a more than presentable addition to the fleet, but never was the winner Foo III had been.

Mason at the helm. (Rapp Collection)

The 22-square-meter crews of the 1940s and 50s comprised a fleet to remember. Many members had something to do with architecture and design, as often seems the case among racing sailors. One reason has to be that sailboats present a graceful form of moving architecture, especially when running before the wind under mainsail, genoa jib and full balloon spinnaker. Maybe too it is the steely strategy behind the open competition of racing under sail, since architects and designers, no matter how outwardly pleasant, are used to workday lives in fierce but quiet professional gamesmanship. Or maybe it's the numbing technical minutiae of aspect ratios, ratios of weight to friction, topside heights and surfaces, keel weight, tumblehome stability, centers-of-effort relative to center lines, centers-of-moment (in which a hull's weight in motion is in suspension, called "planing") and other arcana you have to love before you can know.

These sailors took their competition seriously, and at the beginning of each race, as the boats vied for position at the starting line, the tension was palpable. The starting line of the usually triangular

Mason Rapp's most winning 22-square-meter Foo III in high performance off the Adler Planetarium, Chicago. (Rapp Collection)

Rapp & Rapp's chief draftsman Charles A. "Mac" McCarthy joined the fleet of 22s at Chicago Yacht Club with Naia. Mac is at the helm. (Rapp Collection)

racecourse was established between a marker at one end and the race committee boat named Carrier at the other. Timing was everything, all based on the five minute gun and the one minute gun fired aboard Carrier. Skippers synchronized their stopwatches according to the smoke from the gun and not to the deceptive sound of the report, which was delayed over distance. Crossing the line with full sails just with the puff of smoke from the starting gun was a fine art. If a skipper crossed too soon he had to come around again, which often meant he had lost the race before he started. Skippers who were too slow in crossing the line forfeited critical seconds. The melee at the start could be crowded, noisy and even dangerous; but it was beautiful to see.

Mason Rapp's reports back at the office of the glories of sail enticed Charlie McCarthy to buy a 22 of his own, called Naia (S-14). Mac became an analytical and quietly determined club course racer who never seemed to get rattled. Wearing his characteristic long-billed ball cap, his habit at the tiller was to slump in the cockpit to better watch the trim of his sails. He trained his crew in the same way he instructed his draftsmen with quiet repetition and patience. The temperamental opposite of McCarthy was Edmund Sheehan, who used Vinst (S-246) like a weapon to secure his many victories. Vinst was a big, heavy 1941 Knud Reimers design with which Sheehan liked to force his rights-of-way and bluff his overlaps like a sea-going bulldog. He held the fleet record for post-race protests, which he pressed vigorously. He claimed that he would never jibe around to pick up any crewmember who went overboard during a race. He was never tested in this, but he was never doubted. Ashore Sheehan was a lot nicer and made his living as a private contractor and interior designer.

Two of the best 22 skippers of the day were Richard Latham aboard Svalan and Franz Wagner with his 36-foot Eklund-designed Britta. Wagner in 1945 ran the Chicago industrial design office of Raymond Loewy, most famous in the industry for fashioning the bullet-nosed Studebaker automobile of the late 1940s. Wagner hired Latham as a young designer trained at the Armour Institute under Mies van der Rohe. He also hired a wiry, mild-mannered Dane named George Jensen (not related to the Danish silverware designer Georg Jensen, 1866-1935). Wagner later went out on his own as an industrial designer, as did Latham when he brought George Jensen with him and founded the firm of Latham, Tyler & Jensen. They all met success in what was then a new and fast growing field of industrial design, intent on bringing visual appeal to everything from toasters to commercial aircraft. Among many other projects, Wagner designed the Caravelle airliner interiors, and Latham in the 1970s was design advisor on the futuristic award-winning Bang & Olufsen audio equipment. A gourmet of ample girth, Wagner had a commanding presence which helped make him effective at selling his professional ideas but, as with Mason Rapp, selling came hard to him, prompting his opinion that "there is nothing harder than being nice for a half hour." Nearly always sailing with Wagner was George Jensen, and these three yachtsmen were almost always spoken of as a formidable racing triumvirate: Latham, Wagner and Jensen. They were the ones to beat.

Another designer in the fleet was Peter F. Bollenbach, who lived as a country gentleman and sports car/motorcycle enthusiast in Barrington, Illinois. He produced decorative precision barometers that were sold by Marshall Field & Company locally and at stylish outlets elsewhere around the country. Rapp & Rapp specified the always enhancing P. F. Bollenbach barometers for nearly every office interior. Bollenbach owned and raced Rush, a high-topsided Reimers design of 1944.

One 22 sailor who was not a designer or always a club course racer lives in memory anyway. Raymond Dodge was referred to with good reason as "Iron Man" Dodge. Lake Michigan can boil up more quickly than the uninitiated might think. Many an ocean sailor has been confounded by this characteristic of the Great Lakes. In one very nasty Chicago to Michigan City race, Ray Dodge's Venus was the only boat among all classes to finish. Quickly at the start of the race the weather became blinding, with roaring winds that split canvas and snapped spars. With zero visibility Dodge proceeded to finish the race he had begun and wondered where all the boats were when he got to Michigan City. They had limped back to harbor leaving Venus the victor by default. Rough weather seemed to find Ray Dodge, as at another time he was out with only his daughter as crew. When the weather blew in, Dodge was washed overboard in a sweep of foam. His daughter feared him lost but managed to bring Venus to harbor alone. Unbelievably to his grief-stricken daughter and everyone else, Iron Man Dodge had managed to swim ashore and walk drenched into the Belmont Harbor clubhouse.

Dodge proved himself handy in other ways. Aside from Venus, he owned a cabin cruiser with which he was able to tow a string of 22s to winter berths at Grebe's or Karas's boatyard on the Chicago River north branch. This was a sorry sight—the motorless 22s following along behind a stinkpot, disarmed and powerless with their masts lashed fore-and-aft on deck. Humiliating as this parade may have seemed, it was a practical solution. Before that, every 22 skipper would sail in his own time to the mouth of the Chicago River and remain under sail or lash-on an outboard motor to pass through the locks and up the river. Each tall mast required tenders to raise the many river bridges, stopping overhead auto traffic while the haughty boat passed below. With Ray Dodge's help, all the masts could be pulled at Belmont and the boats towed without incident under the bridges.

These men and others among them in the 22 fleet provided the moving spirit of Chicago Yacht Club at the time. Its skippers were an enthusiastic, boisterous collection of individuals brought together by a love of racing, a desire to win and an overall gentlemanly sense of sportsmanship. Drinking aboard boats before and during races was never done, but the liquor-oiled post race gatherings around the second deck bar of the Belmont club were smoky and raucous.

Those pure old days of wooden boats and iron men began to change when in 1955 Latham and Wagner brought in the first fiberglass Udell class, one-design 22-square-meters by the prolific Knud Reimers. One-designs meant uniform hull configurations from one boat to the next, a conformity made necessary by economics. Latham's Windjak (U-1) and Wagner's Kona (U-2) were beautifully conceived and easily victorious over most of the older 22s. Victory in the club course races became a virtual seesaw between Latham and Wagner.

At the same time, Chicago Yacht Club was getting a new downtown Monroe Street Station club house designed by Rapp & Rapp. McCarthy did the drafting, Franz Wagner the inviting dining room interior design, and CYC member Sumner Sollitt was the general contractor. CYC still had the Belmont Station as the racing sailors' club, the whole first deck of which was given over to sail lockers and gear, but the new club at the foot of Monroe Street brought modern low-key class. After an exploratory crawl with the wharf rats among the creaking pilings of the old clubhouse, Mason came up with a scheme whose main idea was to open it all up and give it light. The plan took full advantage of the harbor view and Chicago skyline by using exterior walls of floor to ceiling glass on three sides. Rather than a collection of rooms and hallways, the interior became areas of space seamlessly connected to one another. In the 1960s when Richard Latham was CYC commodore, the club's lounge area was enlarged while the old Belmont Harbor Station interior was redone to a George Jensen design supervised by Edmund Sheehan.

Rapp & Rapp designed the Monroe Street club at the midpoint of the 1950s, the first undoubtedly prosperous decade for Rapp & Rapp since the 20s. Much of the success had to do with the proliferating automobile, first with drive-in theatres, second with drive-through banks. The king of drive-in theatre design had to be Los Angeles architect S. Charles Lee, another Armour Institute graduate and an alumnus of 1920s Rapp & Rapp, where he learned theatre design from the masters. Outdoor theatre use in the Midwest was limited by the seasons, but Lee had southern California weather where his art deco drive-ins were a year-around proposition. Nonetheless, Rapp & Rapp built three of them: in Niles, Michigan; Hammond, Indiana; and a final one in Milwaukee for Alex Manta, formerly of Warner Brothers. Drive-ins were no movie palaces, but they did require some special handling, like careful grading and drainage to assure sight lines and avoid flash flooding.

Carved out of a cornfield, the Niles outdoor went up close after WWII when building materials were expensive, scarce and sometimes unavailable. Rapp & Rapp met this challenge with the return to the office of an architect from the University of Illinois named Robert K. Bauerle. He had helped supervise the Toledo Valentine job before he was called to serve in New Guinea, laying down airstrips as an officer in the Army Corps of Engineers. Most of the soldiers serving in that fetid climate, including Bauerle, contracted liver flukes, which army medics discovered they could cure by lacing Kraft caramels with just enough arsenic to kill the parasites but not enough to kill the patient.

Bauerle brought back from New Guinea more than the lingering effects of liver flukes. Just home in his Chicago apartment, he unpacked a souvenir parachute silk to show his wife and a fourteen-inch New Guinea millipede darted out. With a machete Bauerle hacked it into three moving pieces, which he dispatched with his combat boots. Back at Rapp & Rapp he proved as resourceful. Mason was worried about how to find cost-effective superstructure material for the Niles outdoor's screen tower. In New Guinea Bauerle had used so-called Bailey bridges made of prefabricated steel sections, which the Army engineers laid down for vehicle traffic over water or bad terrain. After the war the Army had tons of unwanted Bailey bridge sections stored as surplus. Bauerle knew where they were and how to get them at a cost of next to nothing. After that it was a simple matter to cover the Bailey bridge screen tower skeleton with a decorative skin. Attracting traffic to drive-in movies proved so successful that Rapp & Rapp carried the auto-friendly principle over to drive-through banks, and even an innovative automatic car wash building for south side entrepreneur James Coston. At the same time, Rapp & Rapp renovated the south suburban Beverly Theatre for Coston, a former executive for B&K and Warner Brothers theatre manager in charge of the Rhodes Theatre when Rapp & Rapp built it in 1937.

The idea of drive-through banking was sold as a way to increase bank business by offering more customer convenience, and at the dawn of the auto-obsessed 1950s the idea made sense to management at Chicago's South Shore National Bank. Rapp & Rapp didn't invent the concept (the first installation in the country was done by another architect in 1946 for Chicago's Exchange National Bank) but they developed, adapted and perfected the idea starting in 1953 with South Shore's extensive interior renovations and a three window drive-through facility that became the talk of the banking industry.

In 1956 the nearby National Bank of Hyde Park presented a bigger challenge. The bank's adjoining property was a dead-end into a neighboring brick wall, only wide enough for two traffic lanes. This meant cars could access the entry and drive-in windows but would have no room to turn around into the exit lane. This was a serious impediment, but McCarthy, Mason and Storako worked up the idea of a turntable sunk into a pit, like those common in railroad roundhouses. Manufacture of the 22-foot diameter turntable required 14 sheets of drawings produced by Macton Machinery Company of Stamford, Connecticut, done to Rapp & Rapp specifications. Triggered by a photoelectric control system, the turntable rotated cars comfortably in a semicircle and pointed them into the exit lane. The turntable solution was applied again for the Fidelity Savings Bank in Antigo, Wisconsin.

These timely bank projects continued as a niche specialty for Rapp & Rapp in much the same natural way the earliest vaudeville houses worked for C. W. & Geo. L. Rapp. Work proceeded for Chicago's Mid-City and Lincoln National banks; Rock County Bank in Janesville, Wisconsin; the Mercantile National Bank in Hammond, Indiana and others in Illinois and Wisconsin. In the spirit of the times, the old prison-bar teller windows gave way to customer friendly open counters. Bank executives were brought out of their remote offices to occupy desks in view of the lobbies. Warm carpeting replaced the old cold marble floors, and nice seating areas for patrons gave a living room feel to once intimidating environments. On budget and client-focused, this was architecture on a human scale.

13 | MODERN TIMES

The 1950s were good to Rapp & Rapp even as the living links to the beginning continued to fall away. Mary P. R. Rapp in 1947 left Chicago and returned to her home state of California. She moved into a sunny Carmel bungalow near her nephew and frequent traveling companion Franklin Brewer, who was with her at C. W. Rapp's bedside when he died in 1926. Franklin handled her financial affairs and she lived a comfortable life that ended after she developed breast cancer. She died in 1950, having outlived her husband by nearly a quarter century, never foreswearing the solemn black she wore in his memory. Through the ordeal of her illness she never complained and stayed in touch by letter with Mason's wife Virginia; her only regret being, she wrote, that she couldn't come to see Virginia's new house. She had been a frequent guest at the former home and on one visit used the fireplace to burn her personal papers, including packets of letters she and C. W. Rapp exchanged through the years.

A year later, in 1951, Mason's Uncle Charles died in Trinidad's San Rafael Hospital, which had been built by Charles's brothers Ham and Will. Charles Robert Rapp had been steward of the Rapp interests in Trinidad, working from an office in the Turner-Ford Building, which Will had bought in 1906. The Rapp firm had moved there in 1925 from the Masonic Building across Main Street. Charles regularly forwarded shares of rental income from the McCormick, Turner and White Front buildings to Will Rapp's widow Mary and to Mary P. R. Rapp in Chicago. Payments sometimes came up short during the Depression when rents fell behind even as roofs and boilers needed service, all for which Charles carefully accounted. He was buried in Trinidad's Masonic cemetery near I. H.'s grave.

Mase with his brother William Hamilton (Bill) Rapp went west for the funeral, as they did again three years later for after Charles' widow Helen, the last family member in Trinidad, died in 1954.

Mason's brother Bill, younger by ten years, died just four years later in Chicago at age 42. The effects of his polio and the surgeries he endured challenged him all his life. He met all this with a happy stoicism that made him seem fearless. He owned a little Lightning class sloop which he sailed by himself without a care out of South Shore harbor. When Bill was a Todd School boy in Woodstock, Illinois, Coach Roskie made him manager of the sports teams, and he sometimes did heavy physical work with never a call for help. Victims of the early twentieth century polio epidemic often seemed to transform affliction into determination.

After Charles Rapp's death in Trinidad his property management duties for the family's absentee land-lords were transferred to a real estate man named Damian P. Ducy, who ran Steel City Investment Company in Pueblo. With no major league baseball team west of the Mississippi in those days, Ducy was a great Chicago Cubs fan. Whenever he was in Chicago Mason took him to a game. Over the years the Rapp properties in Trinidad were sold off slowly as opportunities arose. Following Ducy's death his son-in-law Bret Kelly at Steel City continued to manage sales of the remaining properties in Trinidad, often out of loyalty at no charge even after Mason Rapp's death until the last niggling matters were closed in the 1980s, a century after Isaac Hamilton Rapp arrived in Colorado.

Mary P. R. Rapp left to Franklin Brewer her share of the Trinidad properties she inherited from C.W., which she claimed had always paid her rent. Considering all that Franklin had done for her, this seems small compensation given the size of her estate, of which a third went to the Red Bluff, California, Episcopal Church her mother had founded. To include her late husband in the church bequest, it was given in the name of Mary Ward Rapp. She remembered members of C. W.'s family with equal cash bequests, while the considerable residue went to her sister, Franklin's mother, in Moylen, Pennsylvania. As executor, Franklin saw that Mary P. R. Rapp's remains according to her wishes went to Moylen for burial.

Separately, Mason's mother Mary Gerardi Rapp (Grandmary) had been plagued by profitless land near Las Vegas, New Mexico, that she inherited when Will died in 1920. By the 1940s it was occupied by two tenant farmers who never paid their rent and constantly squabbled over water rights. Through Pueblo lawyers McHendrie & Pointer she sold the property to the federal government at the outbreak of WWII. Grandmary, always more practical than sentimental, believed the Trinidad area in which her husband had so much faith had fallen into an economic depression that would last as long as she might live. She stopped paying taxes on Will's outlying coal property and before that refused to invest in her brother Vince's optimistic speculation to extract residual gold from the fairly played-out Lexington Mine he had bought near Elizabethtown, New Mexico.

In the midst of all these passings and transitions Rapp & Rapp continued in the sweep of changing times. Modernism was afoot, which meant not only a look but an attitude. People in business and industry wanted to "feel" modern as America cleaned away war and depression. The talk was of being up-to-date and of keeping up with the times. Money may still have been hard to come by but at least it was coming. Open-ended optimism had been away since the 1920s and now it was back.

The 50s fear of becoming passé spilled over into the theatre business, under assault by television. Balaban & Katz sensed power in the small screen and operated the new WBKB-TV in Chicago. Most stage shows had left the movie palaces at the end of the 40s to be replaced by new and

In the late 1940s and early 50s the wide-screen Cinerama process was literally the biggest thing in movies. Rapp & Rapp installed Cinerama in Chicago's Eitel's Palace and the Ambassador Theatre in St. Louis. (Rapp Collection)

"The biggest new entertainment event of the year." - LIFE

spectacular big-screen cinema technology that helped pull people out of their living rooms and back to movies. Most complex of these was the Cinerama process, requiring three synchronized projectors to fill a large concave screen with breathtaking images. Rapp & Rapp was hired to install the process in the St. Louis Ambassador Theatre and Eitel's Palace in Chicago. They devised ways to mount the screen clumsily but workably in front of the proscenium arch with the projectors mounted center, left and right at the front of the balcony. Cinerama was so specialized and expensive that it was limited to only a few theatres around the country, but another wide-screen process called Cinemascope could be introduced into most existing theatres with minimum cost and effort. This process, which Rapp & Rapp installed in a number of houses, required only a wide screen and single projector equipped with an anamorphic lens which squeezed the picture from top and bottom into a panorama. The office brought still another big-screen process called Todd-AO to the Civic Theatre in the Civic Opera House building, designed in the 30s by Graham, Anderson, Probst & White, and installed similar technology into Chicago's McVickers Theatre in 1955. The McVickers, an 1891 Louis Sullivan design, had been transformed into a movie palace in 1930.

The fancy of 3-dimensional movies requiring theatre patrons to wear disposable "3-D" glasses needed little architectural help, but Rapp & Rapp provided it for the Chicago Theatre in 1953 along with interior alterations. There is no way to claim that these renovations were an improvement over the classicism applied by Mason's uncles, and with some justification the changes were criticized in the 1970s by theatre preservationists for having spoiled the purity of the original. In the early 50s, B&K management was trying to adjust to the new reality of television emptying movie houses. Like nearly everyone else in business at the time, they were deathly afraid of seeming old-fashioned.

By 1953 the Chicago had seen more than thirty years of movie-going traffic. During that time draperies and carpeting had gotten tired, floors were greasy and sticky from spilled food, seats were torn, art work that hadn't been stolen or defaced was removed for protection by the management or sold in Chicago galleries, and floor to ceiling graffiti covered the restroom walls. Moviegoers took the old Rapp & Rapp treatment for granted, and B&K management wanted something more modern. To this end Mase and the office put false ceilings in some of the foyers to lower the overhead level and cover the coffered ornament above. Old lobby drapery was removed and replaced with contemporary hangings and, since most of the revenue came not from box office tickets but from food, the concession counter was enlarged and modernized. Along with the new big-screen, a state-of-the-art sound system was installed.

In the late 60s, a few people in various cities across the country began to appreciate anew the theatrical glories Rapp & Rapp had wrought a half-century before. In Chicago, volunteers began to recapture the faded elegance of the Chicago Theatre, and were relieved to find all the old plaster ornament still securely in place behind the 50s false ceilings and other cover-ups. Rapp & Rapp had given Balaban & Katz management their 1953 clean-up and renovation while behaving with restraint, something another architect might not have done. Mason was known to have gutted some movie palaces in the name of progress (the Valentine and the Fisher) but he never seriously affected a Rapp & Rapp.

'Despite Rapp & Rapp's effort to do no irreparable harm to the Chicago, Mason was concerned for the future of the big palaces. Noting the continuing incursion of television and the growth of other recreational activities, he believed the economics of property values ultimately would work against the houses his uncles and other architects had built during the golden age. In a speech he gave in 1962 at Chicago's Hotel Sherman before members of the Equipment Dealers and Manufacturers Association, Mason predicted: "Future theatre centers will contain versatility of exhibition either in single or multiple theatre units, and (will be) located not in but near downtown metropolitan areas with facilities that recognize this automobile age." In a sense it was the good news of a rapidly expanding post-war economy in the 1950s that seemed to translate into bad news for the big movie palaces of the 1920s, and Mason believed the grand theatres would fall away one-by-one. For a time, he seemed right. Many palaces did fall away without fanfare, including Rapp & Rapps' sumptuous Chicago Tivoli in 1963; and in New York in 1964 the theatre portion was gutted-out of Rapp & Rapp's Times Square Paramount Building. Many houses that remained through the 60s and 70s survived by selling tickets to pornography and films of mindless violence. Some of the bigger houses became venues for rock concerts, dope smoking and sex in the balcony. The Chicago Uptown foyers were used as open urinals.

One encouraging sign was the successful 1968 conversion of Rapp & Rapp's St. Louis Theatre into Powell Hall, a new home for the St. Louis Symphony Orchestra, praised by New York Times architecture critic Ada Louise Huxtable. Mason didn't foresee the gathering influence of other forces; particularly those few theatre historians and preservationists who saw real value in magnificent 1920s movie houses and helped raise public awareness about new ways to use them.

Because of these theatres Rapp & Rapp is most remembered in formal terms as "assembly architects" denoting designers of large public spaces, but the firm was drawn ever further afield in the busy, prosperous and quickly changing 1950s. Less romantic than movie palaces but effective just the same were, among many others, a plant addition for Burny Brothers bakery, assembly plants for Vacuum Ceramics, garage additions for Imperial Trucking, a laundry building for Roscoe Overall Service and, coming out of the La Salle job, hotel renovations for the Faust in Rockford and the Monterey in Janesville, Wisconsin. As commercial air travel continued to replace passenger rail service Rapp & Rapp designed the Air Line Pilots Association office building at Chicago's Midway Airport, followed by consulting jobs for other ALPA buildings around the country. United Air Lines hired Rapp & Rapp to design ticket and reservations offices at Midway and four downtown Chicago locations, as did Eastern Air Lines for Midway terminal alterations. A simultaneous alteration was done for Continental Trailways' downtown Randolph Street bus terminal.

During these years Sigma Chi Fraternity reconnected with Rapp & Rapp for alterations and additions to C. W. & Geo. L. Rapp's 1910 Kappa Kappa chapter house at the University of Illinois followed by alterations to the lakefront Sigma Chi national headquarters building near the Northwestern University campus in Evanston. The headquarters director was Merrill Prichard, a journalist from the University of Illinois who, just out of college in 1948, became editor of Sigma Chi publications. He followed on as operations vice president of C. P. Clare & Company, a manufacturer of electrical components and a significant Rapp & Rapp client. Carl Peter Clare, a Sigma Chi and electrical engineer from the University of Idaho, was company president.

With director of manufacturing Herbert Peterson, Clare started his firm on Chicago's northwest side in 1937, fabricating components for Bell Telephone and developing relays for the first electronic racetrack odds boards. By the 1950s Clare's increasingly precision electrical relays called for a cleaner, climate-controlled manufacturing environment, which meant, in short, an entirely new plant. The selected site was in a quiet, mostly residential area on Pratt Avenue at the north edge of Chicago. In those days before landscaped corporate campuses, area residents were outraged at the prospect of a factory in their midst. Clare mounted a huge public information campaign requiring endless local zoning meetings to present architectural plans from Rapp & Rapp along with reams of data explaining the clean and quiet nature of his business and his proposals for park-like landscaping. The main curiosity and selling point was the nature of the building itself, which presented a low, sleek perspective of exterior hard-burned white brick, windowless for interior cleanliness except for glass at the main vestibule entry accented by green ceramic glazed tile. The Clare plant's profile of just 13 feet 10 inches from grade level to roof line seemed to emerge futuristically from the earth, its windowless expanse appearing out of touch with Mies van der Rohe's Chicago structures of the day, which relied heavily on window glass. Built between 1952 and 1954, long before the use of silicon and micro-circuitry, the Clare plant with obsessive concern for cleanliness represented high-technology manufacture at its beginnings.

First 1950s rendering of the of the C. P. Clare plant in Chicago. Clare used this and others to convince the public and local officials that the proposed plant would be clean and unobtrusive. (Rapp Collection)

Carl Clare in his own way demanded from Rapp & Rapp as much quality and function for his new plant as the Balabans had for their movie palaces. His insistence on easy maintenance, which translates to greater cleanliness, meant interior walls of glazed tile, a ceiling of acoustical steel, and floors of asphalt tile that never needed applications of dust-catching wax. Low 9-foot ceilings throughout the plant assured cheaper and better air-conditioning, and to Clare good air-conditioning was less important for the executive offices than it was for the plant assemblers and their product. Indoor humidity was a constant 50 per cent with a temperature of 70 degrees, or 15 degrees cooler than outside. The air was electrostatically cleaned using electronic precipitators. To provide even lighting throughout, Mason and Ed Storako recalled the egg-crate fluorescents used in the La Salle Hotel drugstore four years earlier. Now they got rid of the egg-crate covers and mounted rows of bare 8-foot fluorescent tubes the length of the plant. Without reflectors or grids, the tubing improved employee efficiency by giving-off a bright, even light that cast no shadows, always the same night and day during the three work shifts. Though common illumination today, this was first in the world, and factory assembly work had never been more comfortable.

At the groundbreaking for the Clare plant's 1957 addition were building superintendent Ernie Stevenson, Carl Clare and Rapp & Rapp's Dan Brush. (Rapp Collection)

C. P. Clare's vestibule. (Hedrich-Blessing photo)

Typical Clare plant executive office. (Hedrich-Blessing photo)

C. P. Clare's main entrance with the only windows in an otherwise windowless building. (Hedrich-Blessing photo)

The Super Clean Room—also called the White Room—built into Clare's late-fifties addition. Scrubbed and filtered air inside may have been the purest on earth. (Rapp Collection)

Assemblers at work in the Clare's windowless building. (Hedrich-Blessing photo)

As Clare's telecommunication technology continued to advance into 1957—and dust as always was the enemy—Rapp & Rapp revisited the plant to design an addition whose chief feature, the Super Clean Room or White Room, seemed even more millennial than the plant itself. To facilitate failure-free manufacture of new dry-reed electrical switches and gold-tipped relays for the earliest and highly secret communications satellites, and releases for the three-stage rockets that launched them, this Carrara-glass enclosed dust-free island within Clare's windowless fortress of cleanliness may have been the purest environment on earth. Air inside was cleaned with micro-pore filters, and air samples were taken throughout every day for routine microscopic particle counts. Workers inside wore sanitized white suits, caps and booties, never entering without passing through cleaning vacuums and shoe scrubbers. Any transfer of an item in or out of the White Room was done via double-sealed pass-through doors.

The press opening of the new facility was set for the end of February 1960. At the start of the month, Dan Brush was signing last minute change orders and approving final catch-up specifications when Mase and he drove out to the Clare plant to assess progress and keep things moving along. Brush was suffering a cold and almost decided not to go, but given the job's looming deadline he changed his mind. In the hallway outside the Clean Room, Dan staggered and nearly collapsed. His color ashen, he sat for a while and said quietly to Mason, "I think you'd better get me home." On the drive to Glencoe, Brush spoke little and kept his eyes closed and his head resting back on the car seat. At home Evelyn Brush helped him upstairs and put him to bed. He fell asleep and never awakened. His cold had descended into pneumonia.

Brush's death at 75 meant Rapp & Rapp had lost a partner who went back almost to the beginning, and now only the draftsman McCarthy remained from the early days. D. H. Brush, only in his early twenties when hired by C.W. and George, had worked through the ornamental vaudeville houses and movie palaces, to the modern minimalism of the Clare plant. His main contribution all the while had been enforcing the orderly start-to-finish progress of every job; in a sense regulating Rapp & Rapp's heartbeat. The details of his duties now fell to Mason, Storako and Clara Weirauch Long, who through the years had drawn up so many contracts and taken so much dictation from Brush that she could virtually do it in her sleep. Sleep was what they all would get less of as the Rapp & Rapp clock turned back to the pace of 1925 with a new theatre job ahead in Detroit.

14 | REPRISE

C. P. Clare opened his updated facility in February 1960, and by the following August Rapp & Rapp was at work on Detroit's New Fisher Theatre, knee-deep in the gutted rubble of the 1928 movie palace that was giving over its cavernous space in the Fisher Building. Now with Dan Brush gone and McCarthy alone remaining from the original firm, Rapp & Rapp's biggest theatre project since the 1931 Southtown seemed especially daunting. One man who remembered Rapp & Rapp's theatrical magic of those earlier days was the 73-year-old dean of Motor City showmen David T. Nederlander of the Nederlander Theatrical Corporation, which he founded in the 1920s.

Nederlander, with his theatre manager sons Joseph and James, approached Detroit's philanthropic Fisher brothers with the idea of bringing live Broadway shows to a venue that would outshine anything in the country. The Fishers would own the new theatre and the Nederlanders would lease and manage it. To the rumors that downtown Detroit was in decline, Nederlander responded to a newspaper reporter, "Detroit isn't dying, but we have to give proof to the nation that it is still alive." Nederlander's idea of the perfect spot for his theatrical dream was the movie palace space within the art deco Fisher Building built in 1928 by Albert W. Kahn, Associated Architects and Engineers. The theatre inside was a Mayan realization in the spirit of the cavernas and cenotes of Mayapán and the dripping jungles of central Yucatan; a brooding masterpiece of mood designed by two Rapp & Rapp renegades from the 1920s, A. S. "Bumps" Graven and Guy Mayger. Mayger had been McCarthy's predecessor as the Rapps' chief draftsman. The Nederlanders and Fishers envisioned no mere renovation, but a project stripped to the concrete and built anew. When Nederlander called Rapp & Rapp to outline this vision, Mason replied, "It's a great challenge, and I'd like to help you meet it."[1]

Graven & Mayger's grand lobby for their Fisher Theatre in Detroit, which Rapp & Rapp replaced in 1961 with the New Fisher Theatre. This 1928 design is similar to Rapp & Rapp's favored Chapel of Versailles scheme, except for the Mayan ornament. (Rapp Collection)

Edwin B. Storako working on the Fisher design at Dan Brush's old desk. The office looks the way Brush left it before his death. (Rapp Collection)

Mason G. Rapp during the Fisher Theatre work in 1961. (Rapp Collection)

The aging Fisher brothers involved in the project (Lawrence, Edward, Charles, Alfred and William) were great Detroit benefactors with a seemingly endless supply of money originally earned from the Fisher Body Company, designer of car bodies for General Motors. The family sold Fisher Body to General Motors in 1927 but for years after had at least one family member on the GM board. They formed a company called Fisher Corporation, involved in banking, investments and doing good for Detroit, which at the time of the New Fisher Theatre was a manufacturing colossus, truly the motor city of the world.

As the optimism of the 1950s spilled into the time of the Kennedy "Camelot" in Washington, Mason and Ed Storako still held to a 1940s client-centered cost consciousness that was needless with the Fishers. Mase didn't realize at first that when it came to their theatre the Fishers amounted to a reincarnation of the cost-is-no-object Balabans. Edward Fisher wanted no seat further than 90 feet from the stage, and that every voice should be heard clearly from the stage without sound reinforcement. Lawrence Fisher wanted the place to be so elegant that no man would feel properly dressed in anything less than a tuxedo. C. E. Fisher demanded the theatre be ready for the October 1961 season, little more than a year away. Mason and Storako cautioned about the cost and, given the size of the job and roughly predictable equipment delays, declared the schedule impossible. The Fishers abruptly told them not to worry about the cost, and to run three work shifts if necessary. Given who the Fishers were, the architects were reminded, there would be no equipment delays.

Rapp & Rapp in effect had been handed a signed blank check, and they were willing to use it toward what the Fishers wanted: "The most beautiful legitimate playhouse in the country." The free flow of money into the Fisher project was also a welcome surprise to Broadway lighting designer Ralph Alswang and Chicago lighting contractor M. A. Van Esso, each of whom said it was the only job he had ever known where no one ever asked about cost. With the original 2700 seat movie palace scaled down to 2000 and capable of reduction to 1600 for smaller productions, Mason doubted that the Fishers could make back their investment in 100 years. As far as the Fisher brothers were concerned, the New Fisher Theatre was simply a gift to Detroit.

The Albert Kahn architects helped Rapp & Rapp avoid re-measuring the house by providing Graven & Mayger's original Fisher Theatre plans. Back in Chicago, McCarthy set to work at the drafting table as he always had, but for the first time in years had to hire extra help to keep the pace. Forced by necessity, Clara Weirauch Long smoothed the Fisher job by taking on the phone and mail contact with contractors, a job previously done by Brush. At the same time, Mason and Storako set up a sub office in the Fisher Building, spending increasingly more time there as the deadline closed in. Storako's work ethic especially impressed the Fishers. Even through the last minute flurry he never slowed, stripping down to his undershirt to work through the heat and humidity. The project employed 400 workers around the clock at a cost of 3.5 million 1961 dollars, giving the Fishers even more than they expected.

A common public reaction was that the New Fisher presented a likeable kind of modern architecture. With a more than two-to-one ratio of crowd circulation space over the orchestra floor area, patrons could stroll the lobbies and mezzanine bridge promenade at intermission as if they were in a grand living room. The warmth of the interior came from extensive use of East Indian rosewood and bronze; carpets and seating fabrics of soft gold, yellow and orange; and varied applications of

marbles including slabs of Laredo Chiaro for the lobby walls, Alabama White and Italian Bottocino as inserts for the terrazzo floors, and Best White Cloud for the circular columns. Installed on a base of Alabama White in the center of the main lobby was a polished angular bronze sculpture, called "Josephine" in the Rapp office but actually entitled The Dancer by Edward Chassaing, director of the department of sculpture at the Chicago Art Institute. Overall comfort came from a state-of-the-art, zoned low-velocity air-conditioning system, tucked away with other machinery in soundproofed sub-basement spaces.

Sight lines were clear and unimpeded by virtue of a new deep-pitch orchestra floor, while balcony seats were brought closer to the stage by eliminating cross aisles. The balcony could be tuned for any type of performance by raising or lowering an aluminum grillage using a motor-operated vertical lift. With the grille flown, the balcony gained 475 seats. Moveable wings were installed for adjusting the stage width between 43 and 52 feet, and for films a flown 50-foot silver screen could be lowered in front of the proscenium.

The opening show was a pre-Broadway production of Kermit Bloomgarden's The Gay Life. The musical, based on stories by fin-de-siècle Viennese writer Arthur Schnitzler, went on to New York's Shubert Theatre for a run of 115 performances; but the real show of the Fisher's opening night,

Entry doors to the New Fisher Theatre, located in the Fisher Building's main hallway. (Hedrich-Blessing photo)

In place of movie palace organ screens, decorative panels using the same diamond-oval motif appearing above the lobby entry doors flank the New Fisher's stage. (Hedrich-Blessing photo)

Opening night at the New Fisher Theatre, October 1, 1961. (Detroit News)

October 2, 1961, was the theatre itself. The actors especially marveled at their suite-like dressing rooms as the best in the world. At the extended intermission patrons in formal dress strolled and gawked. Even Lawrence Fisher, who wanted a theatre that demanded tuxedos, went one better by wearing white tie and tails, his way of saying the New Fisher more than met his requirement.

A modern child of its time, the theatre made news well beyond Detroit. Time, Newsweek, Business Week, Interior Design and other trade magazines, and even Hollywood gossip columnist Hedda Hopper, praised its beauty and innovation. The New Fisher even appeared as a backdrop in the syndicated newspaper comic strip Mary Perkins: On Stage. Beyond its immediate notoriety the Fisher influenced the interiors of Avery Fisher Hall at New York's Lincoln Center (1962), designed by Mason Rapp's U.of I. architecture school classmate Max Abramovitz of Harrison & Abramovitz, and the Dorothy Chandler Pavilion in Los Angeles (1964) by Welton Becket.

Behind the congratulations and celebration of the New Fisher opening lurked some dark reminders. C. E. Fisher, the eldest of the brothers, just at his 80th birthday, died days before the gala first night, while Rapp & Rapp's Mac McCarthy, appearing fatigued and distant, was struggling to keep up with the occasion. Strong as ever at the start of the job, Mac became slow and easily confused as the work around him progressed at top speed. On one occasion in Detroit, he collapsed from fatigue and with nothing better at hand had to be laid out on a drafting table. The moment passed and Mac recovered quickly, but for the first time people felt the need to check and second-guess his work. No one, not even C. W. Rapp in the early days, had ever felt the need to do that. It was McCarthy himself who always watched the work of others. But now, though no one spoke of it as anything but temporary, McCarthy's vast knowledge was slipping away.

Back in Chicago the office moved on to other work. McCarthy clearly was less alert and able. With Mase's encouragement he began to spend more time at home. He had been an Olympic skater and a yachtsman, with a liking for his Mercedes Benz diesel automobiles, but McCarthy basically was a simple, quiet man for whom work was his life. Never married, he lived in a south side Chicago bungalow with his two sisters to watch over him. His visits to the office became fewer and finally impossible. Spoken of then as hardening of the arteries, today his condition might be called Alzheimer's disease or dementia. After a while he got to where he recognized no one. The late Dan Brush's son D. H. Brush IV, who used to crew aboard McCarthy's 22 square meter Naia, and as a Chicago stock broker handled Mac's affairs, began paying increasingly futile social calls. Brush IV saw McCarthy through to the end and helped close his estate.

Mac's final absence from the office was a significant event for Rapp & Rapp, far more critical in a practical sense than George Rapp's gradual withdrawal in the 1930s. The office still had Mason, Storako and Clara Weirauch Long, but no one could be expected to follow McCarthy. Efforts to replace him became a revolving door of under-qualified applicants, inefficient temps and outright failures, while young draftsmen showing promise required too much supervision.

Mason went after a proposed bank job in north-suburban Evanston that never was built, followed by a series of small bank, airline ticket office and factory improvements. It was the era of shopping center movie houses, which Mason disdained. C. P. Clare continued in the mix with follow-up alterations to his Mundelein, Illinois, facility, but toward the mid-1960s the pace of building had slowed. Mason always noted that the building business was cyclical. Architecture, he said, was always the first to get hit at the beginning of a slowdown and the first to show life at the end. Another job like the Fisher seemed unlikely, so Mase's question in 1963 was whether to wait out the doldrums or step aside and take up golf, the pastime of the aging competitor. He was only 57, too young it seemed to retire but too old to wait out the business cycle. His thought was to shut the Carbide building office and pursue freelance work, but Ed Storako with a large family was far too young to quit. When Mase floated the possibility of closing, Storako pushed for carrying on the office himself under the name of Rapp & Rapp.

For Mason the dilemma was real. Storako was good at what he did and had invested a lot of time and energy into the firm. On the other hand, he was a designer, not an architect, which would mean he would have to partner with someone who was licensed. These practical considerations aside, Mase couldn't forget that Rapp & Rapp had been a family firm spanning nearly two-thirds of the 20th century. It seemed wrong to consign Rapp & Rapp's future to some unspecified architect, but Storako understandably pushed hard. Before giving his answer Mason needed an alternative, which he found with Rapp & Rapp's steady client United Air Lines, whose management knew Storako well. Storako could come on board as a permanent in-house designer for the ongoing ticket office and terminal jobs that Rapp & Rapp likely would have done anyway. Storako didn't conceal his disappointment but understood Mason's sentiments. He accepted the UAL proposal and went to work there. Clara Weirauch Long signed on with the Joseph P. Bazzoni office, Rapp & Rapp's longtime mechanical engineer.

Before finally closing the 57-year-old firm on June 30, 1965, Mason and Clara took a lot of time sifting through the office and the locker in the Carbide building's basement, examining records, equipment and furnishings that had survived from the earliest days. They rediscovered the stored and long ignored rolls of linen theatre tracings the office had done for the Balabans and the movie studios with household names; bound volumes of photostat reductions of architectural theatre drawings harking back to the Al. Ringling and even before; black leather-cased mechanical drawing sets that belonged to grandfather Isaac Rapp and Mason's father Will; and volumes and envelopes of professional photographs recording work progress and finished views of the grandest movie palaces in the world.

The office had discarded many of the original linens in 1930 when the photostat reductions were made, retaining complete sets of drawings only for the jobs they believed might yield future work, including the Chicago Theatre, Oriental Theatre and Bismarck Hotel, Washington, D. C.'s National Press Building, and Brooklyn's Loew's Kings, chief among others. Most routine office records and working drawings had been discarded by C.W. and George during the move from the Title & Trust Building to the State-Lake in 1918, and more was jettisoned before the next move from the State-Lake to the Carbide Building in 1940. Beyond that, some of the ignored remaining records had been damaged when the Chicago River flooded the Carbide's lower level.

On the final day, with the movers and salvage people gone, only Clara's now dead switchboard remained. Mase and she gave the empty office a final walk-through and took one last look out the windows over Michigan Avenue. Outside the office door Mase took out his keys but lost his nerve. He handed them to Clara and said, "You lock it up."

15 | LAST WORDS

Fifty-eight years after the Chicago office opened, 74 years since I. H. & W. M. Rapp began in Colorado, and 110 years following grandfather Isaac's first work in Carbondale, Illinois, it all came down to Mason. It was a long run, encompassing projects ranging from routine alterations to grand edifices, each pursued with diligence. But it wasn't quite over. Rapp & Rapp was gone but Mason continued to work from his home office under the letterhead "Mason G. Rapp, AIA" followed by the subheading "Formerly Rapp & Rapp, Architects." He couldn't let it go. The name meant something and he was bound to keep it.

From the Michigan Avenue office he had retrieved the furnishings, rugs and equipment he thought he would need, including his Formica-topped desk that in 1958 had replaced George Rapp's dark original with the Chinese tapestry folded beneath its glass surface. Other utilitarian items retrieved included check-writing, Thermofax and adding machines; architectural journals and publications; Dan Brush's green filing cabinets crammed with job records; a drafting table heavy as a ship's anchor; and the surviving linen tracings, photographs and memorabilia from the old firm as it was when Mason joined in 1929. The surviving articles were brought home to shelves in Rapp's basement office where they remained safe and dry until 1988 when the family donated the Rapp & Rapp Archive to the Chicago Historical Society, now called the Chicago History Museum. Many have wondered at Rapp & Rapp's apparent absent-minded treatment through the years of these articles of heritage, but much that is historic now was to them just the clutter of past work and old jobs.

Relocated into his home office, Mason hired Clara Weirauch Long part time to handle contracts, specs and correspondence. He designed a home for a friend, provided factory alterations with a new marble entry and vestibule for Burrell-Belting Company in Chicago and served as owner's architect for the 1970 Wilmette Bank building designed by Perkins & Will. When he wasn't working

M. G. R.

or playing golf, he took to crafting detailed ship models and painting watercolors, which a friend said looked too much like architectural renderings. To get it right for the models he pored over books on full-rigged ships. During this post-Rapp & Rapp period Mason's mother Mary Gerardi "Grandmary" Rapp died, in February 1968, in a north shore nursing home. With no living Rapp presence left in her home city of Trinidad, her ashes were taken out to Los Angeles where they were buried in Hollywood Cemetery beside her husband Will's remains. He had been gone for 48 years.

For a moment in these later years, Mason reconsidered designing single-screen shopping center movie theatres that were all the rage, but gave up the thought. "There's nothing to them," he said. He also thought better of his scheme to "twin" the Oriental Theatre by extending a new floor from the balcony to the back wall. As bad as that would have been, at least he recognized the coming need for multi-screen venues. At the same time, he was taken by the allure of Florida's Gulf coast, spending winters in Naples. Retired Chicago Daily News columnist Tony Weitzel was down there too, working on the Naples Daily News. Weitzel discovered that Mason had worked on his beloved Southtown Theatre, and ran a series of articles on the many glories of Rapp & Rapp. This inspired

Mase to contact Ringling Bros. and Barnum & Bailey Circus World in Orlando, Florida, with a proposal. The idea was to recreate for Circus World C. W. & Geo. L. Rapp's Al. Ringling Theatre of 1915. There was an initial favorable exchange of letters, but Mason's energy was failing along with his health, and he let the effort slide. His failing began to show in small ways. To a friend, he typed a letter so loaded with errors that the recipient replied, "Next time write, don't type." He painted his watercolors, built complex ship models and spent weeks reading Dudley Pope's Nelson at Copenhagen along with other similarly fat nautical books. He also consumed books on golf, just as he had done with anything on racing under sail when that was his primary interest.

In August 1977, at home in Wilmette, Mase experienced a curious limpness in one hand that he attributed to work he had done using a screwdriver earlier in the day. When the symptom didn't go away he entered the hospital and suffered a second, this time paralyzing stroke. Beyond any practical help from therapy, he spent the last months of his life bedridden in a nursing home. It was never clear to visitors how much he knew, but he became agitated and apparently aware when news was read to him that preservationists were working to rescue the Aurora, Illinois, Paramount Theatre, the luxuriant Paris Fair masterpiece Mason worked on with Arthur Adams in 1931. He seemed to understand. Mason Rapp died on May 8, 1978, five weeks into his 73rd year.

Throughout the Rapp architects' long history that ended with Mason, every Rapp building was very much a product of its economic and historical times, from the rapid development of Carbondale and the Southwest through the booming 1920s, the Depression, and the resurgence during WWII to the post-war perspective. In the earlier years their architecture required importation of the European, whether Gothic fancy in the Victorian excrescences, French resplendence or Beaux Arts classicism. As America became the dominant world power and modernism the world style, the iconic Rapp designs were eclipsed but the firm proved capable of remaining current, with, for example, the Chicago Yacht Club and the Clare plant. Beaux-Arts training instilled elements of classical idealism and craftsmanship in Rapp architects right through to the last one. This can be seen in details of design and construction exemplified in the big theatres, the little Carnegie library at Raton, New Mexico (razed in 1969) by I. H. & W. M. Rapp, and the modernist New Fisher Theatre in Detroit.

The Chicago Rapps' theatre designs were at once customer-driven and insistent on integrity. Underlying the flamboyance of a movie palace was sound engineering: overbuilding for safety and stability, C.W.'s obsession with sight lines, fluency of traffic flow, good ventilation, space for maintenance. Because of these factors, the experience of the ticket buying public was, perhaps subliminally, more than being in a classy atmosphere of faux European and riotous profusion. The worst that can be said of the Chicago Rapps is that they satisfied untapped popular taste.

They were all men of the marketplace and necessarily compromising but were not, at the core, corrupted by it. A building was designed for a definite function, and in some cases the designer owned an interest in the revenue stream. If it did not pay for itself, it was not expected to stand as a monument to the ego of the architect. They accepted the world as it was and worked with the powers that be. From the beginning, a key element in the Rapps' success was the establishment and continuance of personal contacts with clients and participation in civic and social life—from carpenter Isaac in Carbondale to Mason and his contacts as a racing sailor.

The Rapps themselves embodied integrity in dealing with customers, employees, and family. There was a sense of competitive professionalism combined with responsibility, and they tended toward a work ethic that too often, in combination with inborn factors, led to stress, premature illness and early death.

Following Mason's death came a resurgence in urban high-rise architecture unequaled since the 1920s and the modernist expansion of the 1950s. Throughout the 1980s and 90s, postmodern construction flourished in American cities and around the world, while architectural preservationists continued an energetic revaluation of historic buildings, notably including work of Rapp & Rapp. Had Rapp & Rapp still been in business, what sort of work might they have pursued? Surely they would have been involved in preserving and recycling their own theatres for modern use. Might they have contributed monumental entertainment architecture in Las Vegas, joined in the burgeoning industry of new sports arenas or gone after Asian high-rise work and the fantasies financed by petrodollars springing up on the Arabian peninsula? No one can know, but the fact is that the options were not so generous for Chicago's Rapp & Rapp following the 1920s, which helps explain Mason's general ambivalence about his profession. He often mused that he might have been better off doing something else, and he never pushed his children into architecture as he felt he had been. But always there was the nature of architecture itself. Unlike the other two major professions of his time, law and medicine, architecture doesn't deal in pain and suffering. Architecture is aspiration; no pessimist ever hires an architect.

Nor could Mason ever really ignore the work of his grandfather, father and uncles, and the examples they set for him. Preservationists have found that everything Rapp & Rapp did had a reason, and they learned to move cautiously before changing anything they didn't immediately understand. Rapp draftsmen subordinated ego to practicality, tending to design things "loosely" out of consideration for the on-site workman who might have to use a screwdriver behind a door, or a plumber who would need room to swing a wrench. Ease of construction and maintenance were for the Rapps no mere details.

In 1987 the Art Institute of Chicago's architecture curator John Zukowsky, along with German and French curators, created an exhibition reviewing Chicago architecture from 1872, following the Chicago fire, to 1922. This huge collection was the first exhibition in the Musée d'Orsay, a grandly recycled 19th century railroad station called Gare d'Orsay in Paris.[1] Included were two original linen tracings of Rapp & Rapp's Chicago Theatre of 1921, which just made it within the 50-year historical period covered by the exhibition. C. W. Rapp's favored French elegance had returned to the source.

KEY REFERENCES AND RESOURCES

Chicago History Museum
1601 North Clark Street
Chicago IL 60614
www.chicagohistory.org

CHM holds the Rapp & Rapp Archive, the complete collection of remaining drawings and detailed linen tracings from the 1920s produced by the Chicago firm. Combined with office photographs of the renowned movie palaces and projects into the 1960s, this collection provides an invaluable overview of Rapp & Rapp history.

Fletcher Collection
Trinidad, Colorado
719-846-5933

Ken Fletcher's collection is the most detailed source of information on the architects I. H. & W. M. Rapp. Included is complete newspaper coverage from Anthony and Wichita, Kansas (1880–88), Trinidad, Colorado (1888–1930) and Santa Fe (1890–1930). In a twelve-year research project Mr. Fletcher single-handedly rescued the Colorado Rapps from history's receding shadows.

I.H. & W. M. Rapp and A. C. Hendrickson Drawings and Plans.
University of New Mexico
Center for Southwest Research
Albuquerque NM
www.elibrary.unm.edu/cswr

Website contains listings of rare remaining early 20th century Rapp drawings and plans in the CSWR architectural collection. Also represented are drawings and plans from 1937–39 by former Rapp architects Francis W. Spencer and Roy Webster Voorhees. The two worked together after the Colorado Rapp office closed. The materials are listed as part of the Center's John Gaw Meem collection.

Theatre Historical Society of America
York Theatre Building, 2nd Floor
152 North York Street
Elmhurst IL 6012
www.historictheatres.org

THSA is a vast centralized and accessible resource of movie theatre history, photos and artifacts. The work of Rapp & Rapp is thoroughly represented in various annuals and quarterly issues of the society's journal Marquee. The website features a wide selection of available books on movie palaces and their history.

BOOKS OF PARTICULAR NOTE

Brush, Daniel Harmon. *Growing Up With Southern Illinois.* Chicago, Illinois: Lakeside Press, 1944. Reprinted in paperback, Crossfire Press, Herrin, Illinois, 1992.

Goodhue, Bertram Grosvenor. *The Architecture and the Gardens of the San Diego Exposition.* San Francisco, California: Paul Elder and Company, 1916.

Hall, Ben M. *The Best Remaining Seats.* New York, New York: Bramhall House, 1961.

Maycock, Susan. *An Architectural History of Carbondale, Illinois.* Carbondale, Illinois: Southern Illinois University Press. 1983.

Naylor, David. *American Picture Palaces: the Architecture of Fantasy.* New York, New York: Van Nostrand Reinhold Company, 1981.

Naylor, David. *Great American Movie Theaters.* Washington, D.C.: The Preservation Press, National Trust for Historic Preservation, 1987.

END NOTES

Chapter 1

[1] Hall, Ben M., *The Best Remaining Seats,* New York: Bramhall House, 1961.

[2] Chicago History Museum, C. W. & Geo. L. Rapp Job Book 1916–1934, Rapp & Rapp Archive.

[3] "Skouras Brothers Enterprises." *Wikipedia,* the free encyclopedia. Web.

[4] Taylor, Howard Floyd, "John Peter Altgeld." *Encyclopedia Britannica,* Volume 1, Encyclopedia Britannica, Inc., Chicago, 1969.

[5] Wright, John W. D., *A History of Early Carbondale* 1852–1905, Carbondale, Illinois: Southern Illinois University Press, 1977, 117.

[6] Maycock, Susan E., *An Architectural History of Carbondale, Illinois,* Southern Illinois University Press, 1983.

[7] Wright, *A History of Early Carbondale* 1852–1905, 275.

Chapter 2

[1] Brush, Daniel Harmon, *Growing Up with Southern Illinois,* ed. Milo M. Quaife, Historical Introduction, xxii, The Lakeside Press, Chicago, 1944.

[2] E. C. A. Bullock, "Theater Entrances and Lobbies," in *Moviegoing in America: A Sourcebook in the History of Film Exhibition,* ed. Gregory A. Waller, University of Kentucky (Wiley-Blackwell, 2001), 104–106.

Chapter 3

[1] Sawyers, June, *Chicago Tribune Magazine,* Chicago, Illinois, June 18, 1989, 9.

Chapter 4

[1] Theatre Historical Society. *Chicago Theatre, A Sixtieth Anniversary Salute 1921–1981,* Annual No. 8, 1981.

[2] *Chicago Tribune,* David B. Wallerstein Obituary, January 6, 1993.

Chapter 5

[1] Goodhue, Bertram Grosvenor, *The Architecture and the Gardens of the San Diego Exposition,* Paul Elder and Company, San Francisco, 1916, 5.

[2] Renovations, supplement to *Architectural Record,* McGraw Hill, New York, July, 1988, 28–33.

[3] Stover, John F., *History of the Illinois Central,* Macmillan, New York, New York, 1975, 73.

[4] Bunting, Bainbridge, *John Gaw Meem, Southwestern Architect,* School of American Research, University of New Mexico Press, Albuquerque, New Mexico, 1983, 8–9.

Chapter 6

[1] Sheppard, Carl D., *Creator of the Santa Fe Style: Isaac Hamilton Rapp, Architect,* University of New Mexico Press, 1988, 43–44.

[2] *Faces of Protest: Mother Jones,* University of Utah, KUED 7, 2000. http://www. kued.org

[3] *The Maxwell (Beaubien-Miranda) Land Grant and Colfax County War,* sangre.com, 1977.

Chapter 7

[1] Ludwig, Emil, *Napoleon.* Translated by Eden and Cedar Paul, Garden City Publishing Company, New York, New York, 1926, 508–509.

Chapter 8

[1] Harbeson, John F., A. I. A., *The Study of Architectural Design,* The Pencil Points Press. Inc., New York, New York, 1927.

Chapter 9

[1] Tobin + Parnes Design Enterprises, *Paramount Building Time Line,* Tobinparnes.com, New York, New York, 2004.

[2] *The New Yorker,* New York, New York, November 27, 1926, 80

Chapter 10

[1] E. C. A. Bullock, *Cinematreasures.org,/architects.*

[2] Chicago History Museum, *C. W. & Geo. L. Rapp Job Book,* 1916–1934, Rapp & Rapp Archive.

Chapter 14

[1] *The Detroit News,* Detroit, Michigan, October 1, 1961.

Chapter 15

[1] Zukowsky, John, ed., *Chicago Architecture 1872–1922, Birth of a Metropolis,* Prestel-Verlag, Munich in association with The Art Institute of Chicago, 1987, Cat. no. 246

Made in the USA
San Bernardino, CA
15 May 2016